Pasta

Checkerboard Cookbooks

NEW YORK

Adapted from *La Pasta*, by Luigi Carnacina, in the series ''Jolly
della Buona Cucina'' (Series Editor, Luigi Carnacina; Photographs
by Mario Matteucci and Sandro Pagani)

First published in USA 1982 by Checkerboard Cookbooks
Checkerboard Cookbooks is a trademark of Simon & Schuster, Inc.
Distributed by Bookthrift, New York, NY

Editorial adaptation and production by
Accolade Books, Inc., New York, NY

Editorial director: John Kremitske
Editorial consultant: Nancy Parilla Macagno
Recipe editing and adaptation: Pam Rabin, Dale McAdoo
Introduction by: Stephen Schmidt
Layout: Marcia Rizzi
Cover design: Michael Simon

ISBN 0-89673-114-6

Printed in Italy

Introduction

The Many Guises of Pasta —Worldwide Favorite

PASTA: LEGEND AND LORE

Everybody eats macaroni. The word has passed into many languages in many lands; yet no one is quite sure when and where macaroni was invented. "Macaroni" (in Italian, *maccheroni*) may be derived from the Greek adjective *makros,* which means "long," or else from *makarès,* which means "blessed" and refers to the dead, for whom families prepared elaborate banquets in which the main dish was pasta. Or it might also come from the Greek verb *massein,* which means "to knead," and from which Italians get the word *matterello,* a rolling pin of the type used in making fresh pasta.

The fervor with which Neapolitans in particular claim the invention of pasta can be explained by the fact that, no matter who actually originated it, they perfected it so masterfully as to make gourmets' mouths water the world over. It is known that Italian pasta production had developed to an impressive degree as early as the 15th century, when there were pasta manufactories in Liguria, Sicily, Sardinia, and Rome. And wherever else, macaroni was a decidedly popular dish in 17th-century Naples, when the hapless city was ruled by the Spanish viceroys, and we know that it had already become the undisputed favorite dish of the masses of poor.

Italy is a country with a great wealth of popular traditions, regional dialects, and wholly local customs. With boundless imagination, the Italians have called their national dish by an incredible number of different names. When the Italians speak of *maccheroni,* they mean *spaghetti* and *vermicelli* as well, that is, any long pasta shaped like an earthworm (*vermicello*), and not the short fluted type with a hole that most people mean today when speaking of macaroni.

There are other typically Italian variations in the "philosophy of macaroni." Neapolitans like their pasta the way it is naturally, while people from Bologna and the Romagna region think of it chiefly as a base on which to lavish all sorts of tasty dressings, from rich meat sauces and a hundred other delights, all the way down to such "degenerate" inventions as *ravioli* and *tortellini.* Around Genoa, the local inhabitants look upon pasta as a means of making the most of their incomparable fresh basil, and the Piedmontese use it to show off their great truffles.

PASTA IN THE RAW

Pasta is, of course, only as good as the methods and ingredients used in making it. Let us consider some of the requirements for pasta as it comes from the store, so that the cook can better choose the product to accomplish what is not really a terribly difficult task: preparation of a fine, satisfying dish of *pastasciutta.*

Take a look at spaghetti, macaroni, or noodles as they come from the package. Commercial dried pasta should be an attractive amber-yellow color, which shows it has good natural ingredients. It should be smooth, dense, uniform, and rather lustrous. Its consistency should be hard yet with a suggestion of elasticity, so that it holds up well under cooking. If something goes wrong while the pasta is cooking, either something went wrong in its manufacture or it is not made totally of hard-grain durum wheat flour (semolina), and therefore breaks off too easily.

Sometimes, however, the reason why the pasta turns out badly in the kitchen is that some mistake has been made in cooking it. A good cook not only has to know how to choose good pasta but also has to know what to do while cooking it. When pasta is drained, it should still have its amber-yellow color, its taste and fragrance must be pleasing (sourness indicates it had not been dried properly), each strand of long pasta and each piece of short pasta must be sound, with no splitting or any undue surface roughness, and it should have swollen to about three times its uncooked volume. Another important test is to see whether the cooking water is barely opalescent, a sign of good-quality pasta. Now let us see what happens in the delicate, vital period that separates uncooked from cooked pasta.

HOW TO COOK PASTA

Cooking time for homemade pasta varies considerably, depending on the thickness and shape of the dough involved. Freshly made pasta requires much less cooking time than does homemade dried pasta or commercial dried pasta. Thin noodles can be cooked to perfection in a matter of seconds, while heavier pasta may take anywhere from 7 to 12 minutes, or even more, to reach the *al dente* stage—that is, still firm to the bite and chewy.

The kitchenware needed for preparing satisfactory pasta is minimal: a good-sized pot or kettle, tall and preferably rounded on the sides. Never use a pot that is barely big enough just because you don't want to waste time getting out another, more suitable one. The heat supply must be steady, and for draining the pasta you need a simple colander with a handle on both sides.

The proportions of cooking water to pasta weight are the same for both homemade and commercial pasta: about 6 quarts of water per pound of pasta. Experts tell us that haste makes waste. Better to take the time to boil enough water, and better a quart too much rather than a cup too little.

Bring the water to a boil, and add 2 tablespoons of salt per pound pasta. When the water reaches a strong rolling boil (and not before), add the pasta all at once, stirring with a long-handled wooden fork or spoon to keep it from sticking together. A good practice is to put the pasta in the water exactly at the center of the pot, where the boiling activity is strongest.

The other half of the secret is to cook the pasta for exactly the right time. When drained, the cooked pasta should not be gluey or sticky, and each strand or piece should be separate from all the others. Many cooks advise adding a tablespoon of oil to the cooking water to prevent the pasta from sticking together, but this may not be necessary if the pasta is stirred carefully and often from the time it is put into the water. The water is slightly cooled by addition of the pasta, so return it quickly to a rapid boil and cook, stirring continually, until it is al dente. The best system of judging cooking time is simply to follow the instructions on the package, taking the precaution of sampling the pasta about a minute before the stipulated time is up. Such direct sampling while cooking is not an altogether unpleasant task; indeed, some experts claim that this is the only way to really taste the *flavor* of pasta itself, possibly coating it with just a bit of grated cheese.

Once the pasta is done, pour it immediately into a colander to drain. If you cannot tend to it immediately as soon as it reaches the al dente stage, add a ladle of cold water to the pot to slow further cooking, then drain it as soon as possible. As a general rule, pour the drained pasta into a deep warmed bowl, and toss with cheese first (if cheese is to be served with it), then softened butter, and finally whatever the sauce. Pasta should be served immediately, piping hot, and preferably in heated soup plates.

One last important word of warning: You must choose the right kind of pasta for your sauce. Although you might think that the particular combination of pasta and sauce is not all that important a decision, the differences between one form of pasta and another are not only a question of aesthetics but also of flavor. The reason lies in the proportion between surface area and weight. Short, heavy pastas like *penne* and *rigatoni* need substantial, highly flavored sauces, while attenuated types like spaghetti are tasty with nothing more than butter and a generous sprinkling of grated cheese. It goes without saying that the butter and cheese must be fresh and of good quality to obtain the tastiest results.

Let us close this discussion of pasta cookery with a simple, folksy admonition: If you use plenty of water and avoid cooking the pasta too long, or not enough, there should be no problem to serving a good plate of steaming spaghetti, or macaroni, or vermicelli, or. . . .

HOMEMADE PASTA

Many people think that making their own pasta at home must be a long and difficult procedure. Nothing could be further from the truth. A few basic rules and a little regular practice will help you turn out smooth, silky noodles and macaroni and plump ravioli with surprisingly little effort.

The best pasta is made with flour known variously as semolina, durum, or Graham wheat flour. This can be purchased in some Italian groceries and specialty food shops. Using semolina, the ratio between flour and eggs is 1 cup of flour to 1 large egg. Unbleached all-purpose flour is a good, readily available substitute for semolina. For all-purpose flour, use a little less: ¾ to 1 scant cup of all-purpose flour per each egg.

Pastamaking Utensils and Aids

A metal tray mold for making ravioli, along with a circular punch for round ravioli and two cutting wheels.
◁

Two types of rolling pins: a traditional wooden one, and a modern molded plastic one.
▷

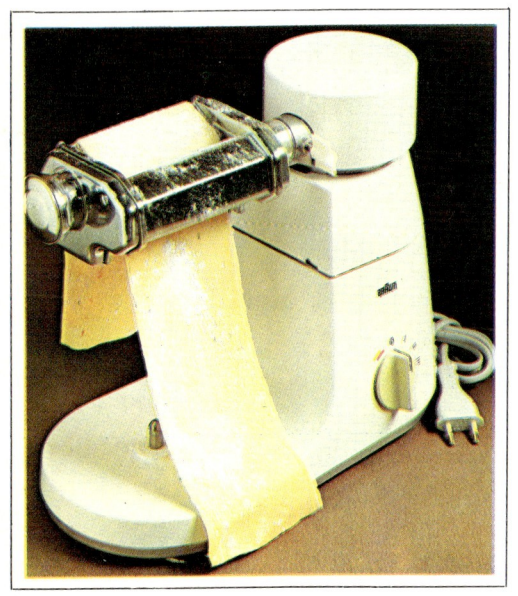

Techniques for making pasta have progressed with the times, and the old-fashioned rolling pin has largely been replaced by various mechanical and electric pastamaking machines. Our grandmothers were experts in handling the rolling pin, adept at rolling out dough over and over again till it became a paper-thin sheet. The electric pastamaker illustrated here has an adaptable motor that powers several different accessories, including the rollers for rolling out the dough and replaceable cutting blades for making the various types of pasta.

An electric-powered pastamaking machine, shown as homemade pasta dough is rolled out.
△

A hand-operated pastamaking machine, in which the rollers are turned by a crank that can be shifted to various positions for changing the type of pasta output. ▷

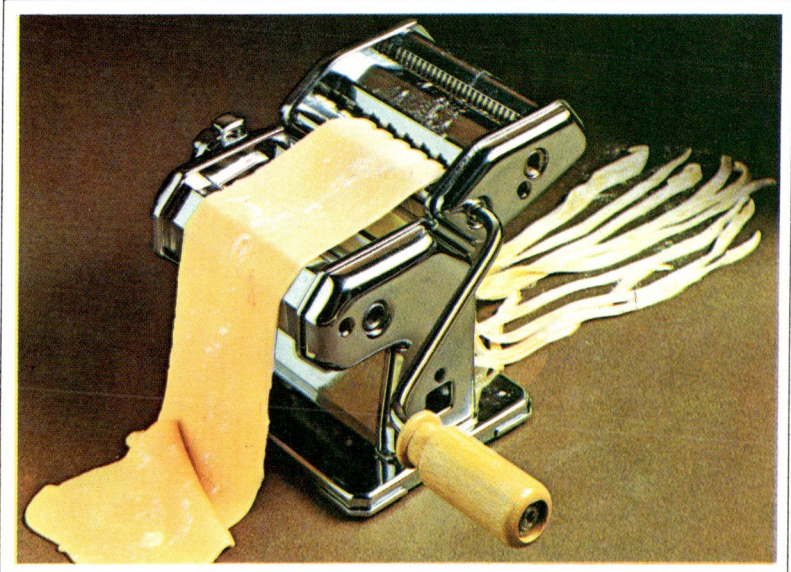

Making Pasta by Hand

Rolling the dough is the most difficult part of the whole pastamaking operation, and the only step that may present some difficulty to the novice pastamaker. First of all, the usual American rolling pin (with approximately 10 inches of rolling surface across) is too short for adequately rolling out pasta dough. A 20-inch French rolling pin available in specialty cookware shops is a much more satisfactory tool; but the ideal-length rolling pin for the task is 24 inches wide. If you have only a short rolling pin, you will have to divide the dough into smaller workable masses in order to roll it.

Both the rolling pin and a large work surface must be well floured. Roll the dough away from you, and do not press it down with the rolling pin. Give the mass of dough a quarter turn and continue rolling, always away from you.

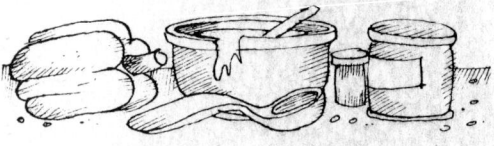

It is important, during the rolling process, that the dough be kept perfectly round and of uniform thickness, between ⅛ and 1/16 of an inch thick. After rolling, let the dough rest for a few minutes, then cut it in the desired lengths or shapes. For noodles, gently fold the sheet of dough back on itself or roll it up loosely, then slice crosswise into noodles of the desired width. Spread the noodles to dry on a cloth or a tabletop, or hang them from a rod, for 5 minutes if they are to be cooked at once, or for 30 minutes to an hour if they are to be stored for later use.

Making Pasta with a Machine

One thing has always been certain: a principal ingredient of good homemade pasta dough is elbow grease, liberally applied with a rolling pin. However, if you're a busy cook who might prefer to direct all that energy elsewhere, good pasta can be made at home with either an electric or a manual machine. As compared with entirely hand-made pasta, you may or may not detect a slight loss in quality; but the gain in time and the lightened labor is undeniable. Any homemade pasta, whether coaxed lovingly into shape by hand or encouraged more forcefully into uniform widths by the rollers of a machine, is still far superior to the dried boxed item.

Pastamaking machines are now readily available in the United States in both electric and hand-cranked models. These vary greatly in size and cost, but all operate on roughly the same principle—to knead the dough as well as roll it out and cut it to the desired size and form.

Generally, the whole ball of pasta dough is divided into six to eight pieces. Each piece is first flattened somewhat by hand (while the remaining rounds of dough are covered with plastic wrap to keep them from drying out) and then run through the machine rollers until the dough is smooth. The rollers are reset, and the sheets of dough are rolled out to the desired thinness. The machine is then adjusted to cut the dough into desired widths. The Bialetti electric pastamaking machine, a particular favorite of homemade pasta lovers, features nylon rollers that give the noodles a very slightly pebbled surface which holds cheese and sauces better than a smooth-finish pasta.

How to Make Cappelletti

1.

Cut a thin sheet of pasta dough into 1½-inch squares. Put about ½ teaspoon of filling in the center of each square. Fold dough squares on the diagonal to make triangles.

2.

Seal each triangle by pinching dough all along the edges. The seal must be a good one so that filling doesn't seep out during cooking.

3.

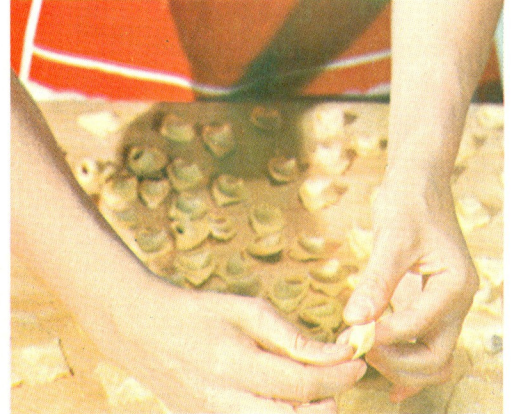

Wrap triangles around index finger of one hand, leaving apex of each triangle free and pushing it upward to give each "little hat" its characteristic form.

4.

Seal the two base corners of the triangle by pressing them together tightly. Set cappelletti on a clean dry dish towel; if not to be cooked immediately, turn them regularly so they will dry well.

Notes on Some Ingredients Used in the Recipes

Capers:
Use small Italian-style capers. If only the large Spanish-style capers are available to you, chop them coarse before measuring.

Herbs:
To substitute dry herbs for fresh, use only one-third the amount of fresh called for in the recipe. Since most dry herbs have a shelf life of only six months or so, jars or other containers should be clearly labeled and dated, as well as kept tightly covered. Marjoram, in particular, gives best results when quite new. Whether fresh or dry, herbs are meant to add both flavor and fragrance to your sauces. Dried rosemary, thyme, and sage leaves should be crushed between the fingers just as they are added to a sauce. (Always use *only* fresh parsley, which is readily available at greengrocers and the produce counters of supermarkets.)

Mortadella:
Genuine mortadella is a delicate-flavored cooked pork sausage made in Bologna, Italy. An American version that is more widely available differs appreciably in flavor.

Mushrooms:
Imported European dried wild mushrooms are generally available in supermarkets. The water in which they are soaked to prepare them for use is very flavorful. When the mushrooms are drained, this liquid should be strained well and added to the mushroom sauce, or else refrigerated and used later for making stock. Dried mushrooms, if stored in a tightly sealed container, will keep indefinitely.

Oil:
A light olive oil is generally recommended for recipes in this book, though corn, safflower, sunflower, and other oils without too pronounced a flavor may also be used. In the occasional recipe purposely specifying olive oil in the ingredients list, the flavor of a good, fruity olive oil is an especially desirable component.

Olives:
Unless otherwise specified, use Italian- or Greek-style black olives, generally 10 or 12 per ¼ pound.

Parsley:
As noted, only fresh parsley should be used, and preferably the flat-leaf Italian variety.

Salami:
Buy the soft, ready-to-eat cooked salami used for sandwiches, usually known in the United States as Genoa salami.

Seasonings:
Bacon, olives, and especially capers and anchovies can be very salty. In recipes including these ingredients, go light on salt and be sure to adjust all seasoning to taste after all the ingredients have been added.

Semolina:
The finest pasta is made wih semolina, a yellowish flour made from hard or durum wheat. But if this is not easily available, unbleached all-purpose flour may be used for pasta dough.

Tomatoes:
When using fresh tomatoes in the recipes given here, peel and core them before measuring. The best canned tomatoes to buy for use in recipes found in this book are the Italian plum variety, usually canned together with some fresh basil leaves.

Glossary of Pasta Terms

Agnolotti: Round or semicircular ravioli, generally meat-filled and made with fresh pasta dough.

Bavette: Narrow noodles about ⅛ inch wide, particularly popular in central and southern regions of Italy; sometimes used also for a pasta similar to linguine in appearance.

Bowties: Also "butterflies"; see *Farfalle.*

Bigoli: A Venetian vernacular name for spaghetti.

Bucatini: Hollow, spaghetti-like pasta that resembles long, attenuated macaroni; see also *Perciatelli.*

Cannelloni: Rectangles of homemade pasta, which are stuffed with varied fillings, rolled, and then baked with sauce.

Cannolicchi: Small tubular pasta, similar to very short macaroni.

Capelli d'angelo: "Angel's hair," an extremely fine spaghetti-like pasta, most often used in soups.

Capellini: Another very fine spaghetti-like pasta, also often used in soups.

Cappelletti: "Little hats," a variety of small stuffed pasta that can either be used in soups or served with sauces.

Cavatelli: Large, curly pasta shells that are sometimes stuffed and baked.

Conchiglie: Any of several kinds of pasta shells, of varying sizes and sometimes grooved.

Crestoni: Ruffled pasta resembling large coxcombs.

Ditali rigati: Very short, grooved macaroni.

Elbows: Curved tubular pasta commonly known as "elbow macaroni," which comes in an assortment of sizes.

Farfalle: Also "butterflies" or "bowties"; small rectangles of pasta with serrate edges, pinched into a bowtie shape.

Fedelini: One of the very finest of spaghettis, even thinner than vermicelli, and often served in broth.

Fettuccine: "Ribbon noodles," one of the most familiar of all egg noodles, about ¼ to ⅜ inch wide; they are sold both as long straight rods and in loosely wound nests of pasta.

Fusilli: Corkscrew or spiral pasta twists, in their most common form looking like a mechanical bolt.

Gnocchi: Italian boiled dumplings made with flour and various ingredients such as potatoes, spinach, and squash.

Lasagne: Very broad, smooth or ripple-edged noodles that are generally used in baked dishes.

Linguine: A flattened type of spaghetti, which resembles very narrow ovoid noodles in long rod form.

Lumache: Pasta "snails," short lengths of thick grooved macaroni, flared at one end.

Macaroni: Italian, *maccheroni;* general designation for a whole class of hollow pasta items, ranging from the tiny cannolicchi and small elbows to large-diameter ziti, and even larger.

Maltagliati: Pasta made by doubling rolled-out dough upon itself and then cutting it zigzag into irregular diamond shapes.

Manicotti: Giant tubular pasta, similar to cannelloni and used for baked stuffed dishes.

Mezzani: Medium-diameter macaroni, which comes in varying lengths.

Mostaccioli: See *Penne.*

Noodles: Some common Italian forms are fettuccine, lasagne, tagliatelle, tagliarini, and trenette.

Orecchiette: "Little ears," small-size pasta shells.

Orzo: "Barley" pasta, resembling rice grains and most often used in soups.

Pappardelle: Very broad egg noodles that are a favorite accompaniment for wild hare sauce in Italy.

Pasta verde: "Green pasta," pasta dough prepared with spinach.

Pastina: Any of several very tiny pastas used in soups.

Penne: "Quill" pasta, hollow pasta cut on the diagonal like a quill pen, which can be smooth-surfaced or grooved.

Perciatelli: Long, hollow macaroni rods somewhat thicker than spaghetti.

Quadrettini: Also *quadrucci;* tiny square noodles cooked mainly in soups.

Ravioli: Stuffed pasta squares, usually made of fresh dough with a variety of fillings.

Rigatoni: Large grooved macaroni tubes about 1 ½ to 2 inches long.

Rotelle: Term used both for "wheel-and-spoke" form of pasta and also for a spiral twist kind like fusilli.

Shells: Various shell-form pastas such as conchiglie, cavatelli, orecchiette, etc.

Spaghetti: The most familiar pasta of all, long solid rods; a thinner variant is called *spaghettini.*

Stelle, stelline: Small star-shaped pasta used in soups.

Tagliatelle: Egg noodles similar to fettuccine, but generally a bit broader, up to ½ inch wide or more.

Timballo: A one- or two-crust pie filled with meat or vegetables and sauced pasta.

Tortellini: Small stuffed pasta twists similar to cappelletti, which may be served in broth or else with a variety of sauces.

Trenette: Narrow egg noodles that are a specialty of the Genoa region.

Trulli: Small pasta wheels, a very local form of pasta.

Tubetti: Thin, squat pasta tubes, like straight macaroni, which can be smooth-surfaced or grooved.

Vermicelli: "Tiny worms," actually a very thin spaghetti, obtainable both as straight rods or as clustered "nests."

Ziti: A very large variety of macaroni, larger than rigatoni, either smooth-surfaced or grooved, and sometimes stuffed for baking.

Homemade Pasta Doughs

Basic Pasta Dough

Yield: about 1 lb

3 scant cups all-purpose flour
3 large eggs
pinch of salt
olive oil (optional)

In a large mixing bowl or on a flat working surface, form the flour into a mound and make a well at the center. Break eggs into the well, and add salt. With a fork or your fingers, work from the center of the well outward to blend eggs into flour and form a soft ball. You may add 1 or 2 tablespoons of olive oil if necessary to make the dough more elastic. Dust your hands with flour and, on a floured board, knead the dough by stretching it, folding it over, and pressing with the heel of your palm. Give the dough an occasional quarter turn. Continue kneading for about 10 minutes, or until dough is smooth and elastic. You may add more flour if dough becomes too sticky, or a drop or so of warm water if it feels too dry.

To roll out the dough, both the working surface and the rolling pin must be well floured. Flatten the ball of dough slightly, then roll it out in a large circle. Keep dough perfectly round and of uniform thickness. The ideal thickness is between ⅛ and 1/16 inch.

Cut rolled dough into desired sizes and shapes. Then dry on a clean dish towel for 5 minutes before cooking.

Approximate widths for some of the most popular noodle types are:

fettucine/tagliatelle	¼ to ⅜ inch
lasagne	2 to 4 inches
linguine	3/16 inch
tagliarini/tagliolini	⅛ inch

Dough for Stuffed Pasta

Yield: for 4 servings

2¼ cups all-purpose flour
3 eggs
1 Tb milk
pinch of salt

In a large mixing bowl, or on a flat working surface, form the flour into a mound and make a well at the center. Break eggs into the well, and add milk and salt. Then proceed as in recipe for Basic Pasta Dough opposite.

Green Pasta Dough
(Pasta Verde)

Yield: about 1 lb

¾ lb fresh spinach (or 10-oz pkg frozen chopped)
3 cups all-purpose flour
2 eggs
1 tsp salt

Trim spinach and rinse well to remove all traces of sand. Cook spinach over medium-low heat, covered, with only the water clinging to the leaves for about 15 minutes, or until tender. Drain thoroughly and squeeze to press out all water. When spinach is thoroughly dry, purée in a blender or food processor, or chop very fine.

In a large mixing bowl or on a floured surface, form flour into a mound and make a well at the center. Break eggs into the well, and add spinach and salt. Then proceed as in recipe for Basic Pasta Dough opposite.

Some Common Pasta Sauces

Basic Italian Tomato Sauce
('Apummarola)

Yield: 4 servings

2 lb plum tomatoes, very ripe
1 medium-size onion, sliced thin
½ cup olive oil
fresh basil leaves
salt and pepper

Core and seed (but do not peel) tomatoes, and chop coarse. Sauté onion in olive oil over moderate heat until golden. (Do not let the onion brown.) Add tomatoes and a few crushed basil leaves. Season to taste with salt and pepper, bring to a boil, reduce heat, then simmer over low heat until thickened, or about 30 to 45 minutes. Garnish pasta and sauce with a little more shredded fresh basil just before serving.

Bolognese Meat Sauce

Yield: 4 servings

1 medium-size onion
1 garlic clove
1 carrot
1 stalk celery
3 Tb oil
2 slices prosciutto (or bacon or salami), diced
1 lb lean ground beef
pinch of basil
salt and pepper
pinch of nutmeg, freshly grated (optional)
1 cup dry red or white wine (optional)
½ cup beef broth
1½ lb tomatoes, chopped

Chop together onion, garlic, carrot, and celery. Sauté chopped vegetables in oil over medium heat until onion is transparent. Add prosciutto and ground beef, and sauté, stirring to break up the meat, until beef is browned. Add basil, salt and pepper to taste, nutmeg, and wine, then cook 5 to 10 minutes, or until wine has evaporated. Add beef broth and tomatoes, and stir to blend well. Cover and simmer, stirring occasionally, for about 2 hours, or until sauce thickens.

Quick-and-Easy Pesto Sauce

Yield: 4 servings

2 cups trimmed basil leaves
1 or 2 garlic cloves (optional)
½ cup grated Parmesan cheese (or Romano; or ½ cup of both combined)
¼ cup pine nuts
3 Tb olive oil
3 Tb butter, melted
salt
black pepper, freshly ground

Chop basil and garlic coarse, and put in food processor or blender. Add cheese, pine nuts, oil, melted butter, and salt and pepper to taste. Blend to a thick purée.

Add enough of the cooking water from pasta to the pesto mixture to make a creamy sauce about the consistency of thick pancake batter. (This sauce is particularly suitable for use with linguine and various types of spaghetti, served with additional grated Parmesan.)

Pork Ragout Sauce

Yield: 4 servings

1 large onion, chopped
6 Tb butter
½ lb pork loin, diced
1 lb tomatoes, chopped
½ cup meat broth
1 bay leaf
1 garlic clove, minced
pinch of rosemary, crushed
pinch of nutmeg, freshly grated
salt and pepper

Sauté onion in butter until transparent (do not brown). Add diced pork, and sauté over medium heat until well browned. Strain tomatoes through a food mill or sieve, then add to sauce, together with broth, bay leaf, and minced garlic. Season with rosemary and nutmeg, and add salt and pepper to taste. Simmer sauce for about 45 minutes.

Boiled Pastas with Sauce

While many gourmets profess to savor the natural flavor of plain, unadorned pasta, for the larger public it is generally the sauce used with it that makes pasta a genuine taste treat. To dress up the relative blandness of the pasta itself, countless delicious sauces have been concocted to use with boiled pasta, making it into that Italian dietary staple, *pasta asciutta*. These embellishments include the many tomato-based sauces, seafood sauces, cream sauces, meat and sausage sauces, vegetable sauces, and the numerous other varied ingredients that can add to the tastiness of basic pasta, ranging from herbs, onions, garlic, and wine to butter, cheese, eggs, olive oil, and fresh basil or parsley.

Some matchless pasta sauces have truly wide renown, and their names are as recognizable as any other great accomplishments in the world culinary roster: for example, *Fettuccine Alfredo* and *Spaghetti alla Bolognese,* or *alla Carbonara,* or *al Pesto,* or *alla Matriciana* . . . and so on, ad infinitum.

There is another very significant consideration in pasta cookery: mating the right kind of pasta with the proper sauce, for the specific combination of the two elements can be all-important. There is an aesthetic component involved, but most importantly the choice of pasta can also affect the flavor and effectiveness of the sauce. Squat, heavier pastas such as shells and rigatoni generally require substantial and very flavorsome sauces as suitable accompaniments. The finer types such as spaghetti, vermicelli, or thin noodles go quite well with lighter sauces, cream sauces, or even simply good fresh butter and a generous sprinkling of grated cheese.

Bowties with Salmon

Yield: 4 servings

1 garlic clove, slightly mashed
2 Tb oil
7¾-oz can salmon
1 lb tomatoes, chopped
pinch of red pepper flakes
salt
1 lb large bowtie pasta (e.g., farfalle)
chopped parsley

Sauté garlic clove in oil until golden, then discard. Break up salmon with a fork, and add to the pan. Cook for 2 minutes, then add tomatoes and red pepper flakes. Crush tomatoes with the back of a wooden spoon and mix well. Add salt to taste, and continue cooking over medium heat for about 20 minutes, stirring occasionally.

Cook the pasta al dente. Add chopped parsley to sauce and remove from heat. Drain the pasta, and toss with half the sauce. Serve the rest at table in a sauceboat.

Perciatelli with Bacon and Tomato Sauce (p. 40)

Fettuccine Alfredo

Yield: 4 servings

1 lb medium-wide egg noodles (fettuccine)
8 Tb unsalted butter
1 cup heavy cream
1 cup grated Parmesan cheese
salt
black pepper, freshly ground

Cook the fettucine al dente, and drain. In a large skillet, melt 4 tablespoons of butter over medium heat. Add heavy cream and continue cooking slowly, stirring constantly until sauce begins to thicken. Stir in a third of the grated cheese, add the cooked fettuccine, and toss gently to coat with sauce. Cut remaining 4 tablespoons of butter in pieces, and blend into noodles with the remaining grated cheese. Lower heat to barely simmer. Sprinkle sauce generously with fresh ground pepper. When pasta mixture is very hot and creamy, serve immediately with additional grated Parmesan on the side.

Fettuccine alla Bolognese

Yield: 4 servings

½ oz (½ cup) dried mushrooms
1 medium-size onion
1 garlic clove
1 small carrot
1 stalk celery
6 Tb butter
2 Tb oil
2 slices prosciutto (or baked ham), minced
2 thick slices bacon, minced
½ lb lean ground beef
2 Tb chopped parsley
pinch of marjoram
salt and pepper
pinch of nutmeg, freshly grated
½ cup dry red wine
1½ lb tomatoes, chopped
1 tsp all-purpose flour
1 lb medium-wide egg noodles (fettuccine)
½ cup grated Parmesan cheese

Soak mushrooms in water to cover. Chop together onion, garlic, carrot, and celery. In a skillet, sauté chopped vegetables in 3 tablespoons of butter over medium heat. When spongy, drain the soaked mushrooms and slice. In a large covered saucepan, heat oil and sauté prosciutto, bacon, ground beef, and mushrooms over medium-high heat until meat is browned. Stir in sautéed vegetables, and cook for 5 more minutes. Add parsley, marjoram, salt and pepper to taste, nutmeg, and wine, then continue cooking until wine evaporates. Strain tomatoes through a food mill or sieve, and add to the saucepan. Combine flour with 1 tablespoon of butter, and stir into sauce. Cover and simmer over medium-low heat for 1 hour, stirring occasionally.

Cook and drain the noodles, and toss with remaining 2 tablespoons of butter, grated Parmesan, and half the meat sauce. Put the remaining sauce in a sauceboat for individual service at table, and accompany with additional Parmesan cheese.

Fettuccine with Beans alla Lucana

Yield: 4 servings

1 lb fresh baby lima beans (or blackeyed peas)*
1 lb medium-wide egg noodles (fettuccine)
1 Tb lard
2 Tb olive oil
3 garlic cloves, minced
pinch of cayenne pepper
black pepper, freshly ground
salt

Simmer beans until almost tender. Cook the pasta. Melt lard in a saucepan, add oil, and sauté garlic over medium heat until golden. When noodles are cooked al dente, drain and transfer to a serving dish. Drain beans while still hot and mix with noodles. Pour sautéed garlic and fat over noodles. Sprinkle with cayenne and black pepper, and salt to taste. Toss gently and serve.

*Dried cranberry beans, Great Northern, or other similar dried beans may be substituted. Soak beans and proceed as indicated.

Fettuccine alla Modenese

Yield: 4 servings

¼ lb freshly shelled peas (or 10-oz pkg frozen)*
8 Tb butter
1 cup chopped tomatoes
salt and pepper
1 sweet yellow or red pepper, cut in strips
2 oz boiled ham, diced fine
1 truffle, sliced thin (optional)
3 Tb heavy cream
1 lb medium-wide egg noodles (fettuccine)
1 cup grated Parmesan cheese

Cook peas in lightly salted boiling water, and remove from heat while they are still slightly underdone. Melt 4 tablespoons of butter in a pan. Add tomatoes and salt and pepper to taste, then cook for a few minutes. Add peas, sweet pepper strips, ham, and truffle. Continue cooking, stirring occasionally with a wooden spoon. Heat the cream, but do not allow it to boil.

Cook the pasta al dente, drain, and toss with remaining butter, the warm cream, the tomato sauce, and half the grated Parmesan. Serve the rest of the grated cheese at the table.

*If canned peas are used, drain liquid and add peas only when other ingredients are well cooked.

Fettuccine with Mussels

Yield: 4 servings

3 or 4 doz mussels
⅔ cup oil
black peppercorns, crushed
2 garlic cloves, minced
1½ lb tomatoes, chopped
salt
1 lb medium-wide egg noodles (fettuccine)
fresh parsley, chopped

Scrub mussels and put them in a large skillet, with 2 or 3 tablespoons of oil and several crushed peppercorns. Cover and cook over medium-high heat until shells open. Detach mussels and discard shells. Strain the cooking juices and reserve.

Sauté garlic briefly in remaining oil. Add broth from mussels, simmer to reduce slightly, then stir in tomatoes, and add salt to taste. Bring to a boil and simmer for 15 minutes. Just before serving, add mussels to the sauce, mixing well with a wooden spoon.

Cook and drain noodles, then toss with sauce and chopped parsley to serve. (Garnishing with grated cheese is not recommended for this seafood pasta.)

Fettuccine alla Piemontese

Yield: 4 servings

oil
4 Tb butter
2 oz fatty boiled (or baked) ham, minced
2 slices lean bacon, minced
1 garlic clove, slightly mashed
1 small carrot, chopped
1 small onion, chopped
1 stalk celery, chopped
½ oz (½ cup) dried mushrooms
½ lb ground beef
¼ lb ground veal
salt and pepper
1 bay leaf
pinch of thyme
pinch of marjoram
dry red wine
1 lb tomatoes, chopped
1 lb medium-wide egg noodles (fettuccine)
½ cup grated Parmesan cheese
1 white truffle (optional)

To prepare meat sauce: Heat oil and 2 tablespoons of butter in a large saucepan, and sauté ham and bacon, garlic clove, and chopped carrot, onion, and celery. Discard cooked garlic. Soak the mushrooms until spongy, squeeze dry, and chop. Add mushrooms, beef, and veal to the pan. Cook over high heat for a few minutes. then season to taste with salt and pepper, and add bay leaf, thyme, marjoram, and a sprinkle of dry red wine. Cook until wine evaporates, then add tomatoes and simmer gently for at least 1 hour.

Cook the pasta, drain, and toss with remaining 2 tablespoons of butter and half the meat sauce. Sprinkle with grated Parmesan and garnish with slivers of the white truffle to serve. Remaining meat sauce can be put in a sauceboat for individual table service.

Fettuccine with Sage

Yield: 4 servings

1 lb medium-wide egg noodles (fettuccine)
½ lb butter
fresh sage leaves*
salt
1 cup grated Parmesan cheese

* Only *fresh* sage will suffice for this recipe.

Cook noodles. Shortly before they are done, melt butter in a saucepan, add several sage leaves and a pinch of salt, and brown the butter. When noodles are cooked al dente, drain and sprinkle them with half the grated Parmesan, pour on the melted seasoned butter, toss well, and serve immediately. Pass around the rest of the cheese at table.

Bowties with Salmon (p. 20)

Macaroni au Gratin (p. 67)

Gnocchi Hungarian Style

Yield: 4 servings

2 eggs
salt
2 cups all-purpose flour
¾ cup sour cream, warmed
4 Tb butter, melted

Beat eggs in a bowl, with a pinch of salt. Add 1 tablespoon of flour, stirring constantly, then continue adding water and flour to obtain a loose, smooth dough that is slightly sticky. Divide dough in small portions; then, on a floured surface, roll each into a cylinder about ¾ inch thick. Cut in segments an inch long or less.

Cook these, about a dozen at a time, in 4 or 5 quarts of lightly salted boiling water. When dumplings rise to the water surface, boil for another minute or two, then remove them with a slotted spoon. Transfer to a warm platter, and garnish with warmed sour cream and melted butter.

Potato Gnocchi with Meat Sauce

Yield: 4 servings

2 lb mealy potatoes
about 3 cups all-purpose flour
1 egg
salt
nutmeg, freshly grated
1 small onion, minced
1 small carrot, minced
1 stalk celery, minced
2 slices bacon, minced
2 Tb oil
4 Tb butter
½ lb lean ground beef
dry red wine
1 lb tomatoes, chopped
1 bay leaf
pepper
1 cup grated Parmesan cheese

First prepare the gnocchi: Boil potatoes in their jackets, peel and, while still hot, pass them through a potato ricer or food mill. Add 2 cups of flour, egg, and a pinch of salt and grated nutmeg to potato purée. Knead the mixture until smooth and only slightly sticky. (If mixture is too thin and runny, add a little more flour.) Divide dough and form into sausage-like rolls about the thickness of your thumb. Then cut rolls in pieces about an inch long. With floured hands, using your thumb, press each bit of dough against the tines of a fork to make a slightly concave shell. Set these on lightly floured surface.

Next prepare the meat sauce: Sauté the minced onion, carrot, celery, and bacon in oil and 2 tablespoons of butter. Add ground meat, and brown over high heat. Baste with a little red wine, reduce heat, and cook until wine evaporates. Add chopped tomatoes and bay leaf. Season to taste with salt and pepper, then simmer for about 1 hour, or until sauce is nicely thickened.

Cook the gnocchi, a few at a time, in plenty of lightly salted boiling water. Remove from boiling water with a perforated spoon as soon as they rise to water surface, generally within a few minutes. Set cooked gnocchi in layers in a serving dish, and spoon tomato sauce over each layer before adding the next. To serve, dot with remaining 2 tablespoons of butter and sprinkle with grated Parmesan.

Spinach Gnocchi with Mushroom Sauce

Yield: 4 servings

1 lb fresh spinach (or 10-oz pkg chopped frozen)
2 lb mealy potatoes
about 3 cups all-purpose flour
1 egg
salt
nutmeg, freshly grated
1 small onion, minced
1 garlic clove, slightly mashed
6 Tb butter
½ lb tomatoes
½ lb fresh mushrooms
½ cup grated Parmesan cheese

First prepare the gnocchi: Cook thoroughly washed spinach in very little salted water. Drain spinach, squeeze out excess water with your hands, and chop very fine. Then prepare gnocchi as directed in the preceding recipe for Potato Gnocchi, adding the chopped spinach to potato purée, along with flour, egg, salt, and pinch of nutmeg.

Next prepare the meat sauce: Melt 4 tablespoons of butter, and sauté minced onion and garlic clove until golden. Discard garlic. Chop tomatoes or pass them through a food mill, then add to the saucepan. Add salt to taste, and continue cooking over high heat until sauce begins thickening. Clean and slice mushrooms, and add to tomato sauce. Simmer gently for 10 minutes, or until mushrooms are tender.

Cook gnocchi as previously described. To serve, toss with mushroom and tomato sauce, remaining 2 tablespoons of butter, and the grated Parmesan.

Squash Gnocchi

Yield: 4 servings

1 large butternut squash (about 2 lb)
1⅔ cups all-purpose flour
1 egg
salt
nutmeg, freshly grated
4 Tb butter
1 small onion, minced
1 lb tomatoes, chopped
1 Tb fresh basil, chopped (or ½ tsp dried)
½ cup grated Parmesan cheese

Preheat oven to 375°. Peel and slice the squash, then place in a buttered ovenproof dish and bake at 350°. When tender enough, remove from oven and force squash through a sieve or mash. Add flour and egg to puréed squash, season to taste with salt and nutmeg, then mix well with floured hands to make a thick, smooth paste.

Melt butter in a saucepan, and sauté onion. Strain tomatoes through a sieve or food mill, and add to saucepan. Season to taste with salt, and stir in basil. Simmer the sauce, stirring occasionally, until somewhat thickened.

Fill a kettle or large pot with water, bring to a boil, and salt lightly. Drop the squash mix into boiling water, a spoonful at a time, to make little gnocchi, or dumplings. Remove cooked gnocchi from water with a perforated spoon as soon as they rise to the water surface, usually after about 3 minutes. Pour sauce over platefuls of gnocchi, sprinkle with grated Parmesan cheese, and serve immediately.

"Hay and Straw" with Tomato Sauce

Yield: 4 servings

3 carrots
½ small onion, chopped fine
1 stalk celery, chopped fine
4 Tb butter
1 Tb oil
1 lb tomatoes, chopped
salt and pepper
hot meat broth
½ lb shelled fresh peas (or 10-oz pkg frozen)
½ lb green (spinach) noodles
½ lb yellow (egg) noodles
grated Romano cheese

Chop one carrot fine, and sauté with onion and celery in 1 tablespoon each of butter and oil until onion is wilted. Strain tomatoes through a sieve or food mill, and add to the saucepan. Season to taste with salt and pepper. Simmer for about 1 hour, stirring occasionally. Add a little hot broth or water if sauce becomes too thick.

Chop remaining carrots coarse, and cook in lightly salted boiling water until almost tender. Cook peas until almost tender. Drain carrots and peas, then finish cooking together in 1 tablespoon of butter.

Cook the two kinds of noodles al dente in separate pots. Drain them separately, add 1 tablespoon of butter to each, and toss gently. Arrange both green and yellow noodles on a long serving platter, with sauce between them and carrots and peas spread around the edges. Sprinkle with grated Romano cheese to serve.

Linguine ai Frutti di Mare

Yield: 4 servings

2 doz clams
2 doz mussels
5 Tb oil
black pepper
1 small onion, chopped
1½ lb tomatoes, chopped
salt
hot pepper flakes
1 lb linguine (or long thin noodles)
1 Tb chopped fresh basil (or about 1 tsp dried)

Scrub clams and mussels, and place in a large skillet with 2 tablespoons of oil and some black pepper. Cover and cook over high heat to open the shellfish. Detach mussels and clams from their shells. Strain the cooking liquid and reserve. Sauté onion and garlic in remaining 3 tablespoons of oil. Strain the tomatoes through a sieve or food mill, then add to the skillet or saucepan. Add salt to taste and a few hot pepper flakes; simmer sauce to reduce slightly.

Cook the pasta. Just before serving, add the shellfish and a few tablespoons of their cooking juices to the tomato sauce. Adjust seasoning to taste, and add fresh chopped basil. Remove sauce from heat. Drain the pasta, and toss with half the sauce. Put the rest of the sauce in a sauceboat for individual service at table.

Fettuccine with Beans alla Lucana (p. 23)

Linguine with Capers and Olives

Yield: 4 servings

1 lb linguine
½ cup oil
2 garlic cloves, crushed
⅓ cup capers
¼ lb (10–12) black olives, pitted and chopped
1 Tb chopped parsley
salt
black pepper, freshly ground
3 to 4 oz chunk tuna, packed in oil

Cook the pasta. Meanwhile, heat oil in a saucepan. Add garlic, capers, chopped olives and parsley, salt to taste, and several turns of freshly ground pepper. Stir in 1 or 2 tablespoons of boiling water from the linguine cooking pot. Simmer sauce for only a few minutes, add tuna chunks, and blend gently. Drain pasta, and toss with the hot sauce.

Gourmet Seafood Linguine

Yield: 4 servings

1 or 2 doz clams
1 or 2 doz mussels
¼ lb small shrimp
pepper
dry white wine
1 small onion, chopped
1 garlic clove, minced
pinch of sage
pinch of rosemary, crushed
¼ cup oil
½ lb squid, sliced thin
1 lb tomatoes, chopped
salt
1 lb linguine
3 oz chunk tuna, crumbled
2 Tb butter, softened
4 anchovy fillets, chopped

Scrub clam and mussel shells with a brush, and clean shrimp. Place clams, mussels, and shrimp in a large saucepan, then sprinkle with pepper and pour in a generous bottom cover of white wine. Heat until clams and mussels are all open. Strain off liquid, discard shells, and return shellfish to their cooking liquid and set aside.

Sauté onion, garlic, sage, and rosemary in oil until onion is wilted. Add 2 or 3 tablespoons of wine and simmer to reduce. Add sliced squid, tomatoes, and salt and pepper to taste. Bring to a boil, reduce heat, and simmer under squid is tender.

Cook the linguine. A few minutes before removing tomato sauce from the stove, add cooked shrimp, clams, mussels, and crumbled tuna. Dilute sauce with a few tablespoons of reserved cooking liquid. Adjust seasoning to taste. Blend butter and chopped anchovies. Drain linguine when al dente, cover with seafood sauce, and dot with anchovy butter to serve.

Linguine al Pesto

Yield: 4 servings

4 cups fresh basil leaves, loosely packed
3 garlic cloves
salt
½ cup grated Parmesan cheese
¾ cup grated Romano cheese*
1 cup olive oil
1 lb linguine (or long thin noodles)

Mash basil leaves, garlic, and a pinch of salt with a mortar and pestle, gradually adding grated Parmesan and half the Romano cheese. When basil has been ground to a pulp, add oil in a slow trickle, stirring constantly. (These steps may also be done using a food processor.)

Cook and drain the pasta, reserving 2 tablespoons of the water. Combine the remaining Romano with the reserved cooking water, and add to pasta. Add pesto mixture, and toss gently but thoroughly. Serve immediately.

* If obtainable, a tasty substitute for Romano cheese in this classic recipe would be imported pecorino cheese.

Linguine with White Clam Sauce

Yield: 4 servings

1 lb linguine (or thin spaghetti)
¼ cup olive oil
1 garlic clove, minced   .
¼ cup parsley, minced
¼ cup white wine (or juice of ½ lemon)
2 7-oz cans minced clams
salt
black pepper, freshly ground

Cook the pasta. Meanwhile, heat olive oil and sauté garlic over medium-low heat until golden. (Do not allow garlic to brown.) Stir in parsley, then wine. Drain clams, adding their liquid to the saucepan. Season to taste with salt and pepper. Simmer very gently over low heat.

When the pasta is cooked al dente, add clams to sauce, and simmer very gently for 3 to 5 minutes, or just long enough to heat them through. Drain the pasta, toss with clam sauce, and serve immediately, with additional fresh ground pepper and chopped parsley for garnish, if desired.

Macaroni with Bacon Sauce

Yield: 4 servings

1 thick slice lean bacon, diced
¼ cup oil
½ lb onions, sliced thin
1 lb elbow macaroni (or rigatoni)
hot pepper flakes
salt
½ cup grated Romano cheese

Sauté diced bacon in oil over medium-low heat. Remove bacon from frying pan with a slotted spoon, and drain on paper towel. Add onions to fat in the pan, and sauté until golden.

Cook the pasta al dente. Add bacon, a dash of red pepper flakes, and salt to taste to the onions. Drain pasta, then toss with grated cheese and onion sauce to serve.

Macaroni with Two Cheeses

Yield: 4 servings

1 lb large elbow macaroni (or rigatoni)
1 cup grated Parmesan cheese
¼ lb butter, softened
½ lb mozzarella cheese, diced
black pepper, freshly ground

Cook the macaroni. Combine grated Parmesan with a little boiling water from the pasta. When cooked al dente, drain pasta, toss with butter, moistened Parmesan, and mozzarella. Season generously with fresh ground pepper and serve.

Broad Noodles with Chicken Livers

Yield: 4 servings

1 carrot, chopped fine
1 stalk celery, chopped fine
2 Tb minced onion
1 Tb oil
2 Tb butter
¾ lb chicken livers
dry Marsala wine
salt
1 Tb tomato paste
½ cup hot broth
1 lb broad egg noodles
½ cup grated Parmesan cheese

Sauté chopped carrot, celery, and onion in oil and 1 tablespoon of butter. Chop livers, and add to the skillet or saucepan along with Marsala. Add salt to taste, then continue cooking for several minutes. Dilute tomato paste in hot broth or water, stir into sauce, and simmer for 30 minutes.

Cook noodles al dente, drain, and toss with remaining tablespoon of butter, liver sauce, and grated Parmesan.

Penne with Ham and Peas (p. 39)

Green Noodles with Peas and Ham

Yield: 4 servings

½ small onion, chopped
8 Tb butter
½ lb freshly shelled peas (or 10-oz pkg frozen)
salt
2 thick slices cooked ham, diced
2 Tb all-purpose flour
2 cups milk
pinch of nutmeg, freshly grated
1 lb medium-wide green (spinach) noodles
2 Tb grated Parmesan cheese

Sauté onion briefly in 2 tablespoons of butter, add peas and salt to taste, then mix well. Cook over low heat, basting occasionally with a little hot water until tender. Just before removing from heat, add diced ham to warm.

Prepare Béchamel Sauce as follows: Melt 4 tablespoons of butter in a saucepan, blend in flour, and gradually add milk, stirring constantly. Bring to a boil, reduce heat, and season to taste with salt and a little nutmeg; then cook, stirring continually, until thickened.

Cook and drain noodles, and toss gently with peas, diced ham, remaining 2 tablespoons of butter, grated Parmesan, and half the Béchamel Sauce. Mix well with a wooden spoon, and top with remaining Béchamel to serve.

Noodles with Prosciutto and Tomato Sauce

Yield: 4 servings

4 Tb butter
1 medium-size onion, chopped
1 carrot, chopped
1 stalk celery, chopped
2 oz prosciutto (or baked ham), minced
2 Tb chopped parsley
pinch of thyme leaves, crushed
1 lb tomatoes
salt and pepper
1 lb fettuccine (or any broad egg noodles broken in pieces)
½ cup grated Parmesan cheese

Melt butter in a large saucepan. Sauté the chopped onion, carrot, celery, and prosciutto. Add parsley and thyme, then cook briefly. Add tomatoes, seasoning to taste with salt and pepper. Bring to a boil, reduce heat, and simmer until sauce is thickened.

Cook and drain pasta; add it to pan containing sauce, sprinkle with grated Parmesan, and toss gently over medium-high heat for a few seconds. Serve in a tureen.

Noodles with Salami

Yield: 4 servings

1 lb fettuccine (or any broad egg noodles broken in
   pieces)
6 oz salami, sliced thick
2 Tb butter
2 Tb oil
pinch of rosemary, crushed
½ cup dry red wine
2 eggs
½ cup grated Parmesan cheese
salt and pepper

Cook the pasta. Meanwhile, cut salami in strips, and sauté in butter and oil. Stir in rosemary. Add wine, then simmer until wine evaporates. Remove from heat. Break eggs into a large serving bowl and, with a fork, beat in grated Parmesan. Season to taste with salt and pepper. When cooked al dente, drain the pasta, transfer it to the bowl with egg sauce, and mix quickly. Add salami and pan juices; toss gently to serve.

Piquant Noodles with Fresh Tomatoes

Yield: 4 servings

4 slices bacon, minced
1 lb tomatoes
1 Tb oil
1 small onion, sliced
pinch of sage
salt and pepper
1 lb medium-wide egg noodles
2 Tb capers
pinch of marjoram
1 tsp vinegar
2 Tb butter, softened
grated Romano cheese

Peel, seed, and chop tomatoes. Sauté bacon in oil until pale gold in color. Add onion and cook until tender. Stir in sage, tomatoes, and salt and pepper to taste. Bring to a rapid simmer, then cook for 15 minutes.

Cook the noodles. Before removing sauce from stove, add capers, marjoram, and vinegar. Drain noodles, toss with butter, pour sauce over them, and sprinkle with grated cheese.

Buttered Noodles with White Truffles

Yield: 4 servings

1 lb thin egg noodles
½ cup butter
salt
white pepper
pinch of nutmeg, freshly grated
2 or 3 Tb chicken broth, hot
½ cup grated Parmesan cheese
1 white truffle, sliced thin*

Cook the pasta. Two or three minutes before it is done, melt butter in a saucepan, and season to taste with salt, pepper, and nutmeg. Drain noodles, sprinkle hot broth over them, and toss with melted butter and grated Parmesan. Garnish with very thin slices of white truffle (or sautéed mushrooms).

*One or two cups of thinly sliced mushrooms, browned in butter, may be substituted for the white truffle in this recipe.

Pasta Twists Island Style

Yield: 4 servings

2 garlic cloves, crushed
4 anchovy fillets
2 Tb oil
1½ lb tomatoes, chopped
salt and pepper
¾ cup chopped green olives
chopped fresh basil
1 Tb capers
1 lb pasta twists (rotelle)
pinch of oregano

Sauté garlic and anchovies in oil, mashing the anchovies with a fork. Strain the tomatoes through a sieve or food mill. Add to the pan, and season to taste with salt and pepper. Cook over medium-high heat until sauce thickens. Add olives, a generous dash of basil, and capers, then simmer for about 5 minutes. Cook the pasta al dente. Drain and toss with the sauce. Sprinkle with oregano and serve.

Pasta Twists with Mushrooms

Yield: 4 servings

¾ lb fresh mushrooms
8 Tb butter
salt and pepper
½ cup heavy cream, heated
1 lb pasta twists (rotelle)
½ cup grated Parmesan cheese

Slice mushrooms thin, and sauté over medium heat in half the butter. Season to taste with salt and pepper. Moisten mushrooms with a little of the cream as they cook.

Cook the pasta al dente. Drain and toss with remaining hot cream, butter, and grated Parmesan. Add mushrooms with their cooking juices, and serve immediately.

Pasta Twists with Tomato Sauce and Sausages

Yield: 4 servings

1 medium-size onion, chopped
1 carrot, chopped
1 stalk celery, chopped
2 Tb butter
2 Tb oil
1 garlic clove, minced
2 lb tomatoes, chopped
fresh basil
salt and pepper
1 lb pasta twists (rotelle)
8 small sausages (Italian sweet or link)

Sauté onion, carrot, and celery in butter and 1 tablespoon of oil. Add garlic, tomatoes, and several basil leaves, along with salt and pepper to taste. Siimmer until sauce thickens.

Cook the pasta. Meanwhile, brown the sausages over high heat in remaining tablespoon of oil. Add sausages to tomato sauce, stir and continue cooking over low heat to blend flavors well. Drain the pasta, toss with sauce, and arrange sausages on top to serve.

36

Linguine ai Frutti di Mare (p. 28)

Linguine al Pesto (p. 31)

Pasta Wheels with Olive Sauce

Yield: 4 servings

½ small onion, chopped
2 thick slices bacon, diced
1 Tb oil
1 sweet green pepper
1½ lb tomatoes, chopped
10–12 green olives, pitted and sliced thin
10–12 black olives, pitted and sliced thin
1 Tb capers
pinch of oregano
salt and pepper
1 lb disk-type pasta (or medium-size pasta shells)

Sauté onion and bacon in oil. Cut green pepper in very thin strips, and stir into saucepan. Strain tomatoes through a food mill or sieve, then add to pan, along with green and black olives, capers, oregano, and salt and pepper to taste. Simmer the sauce gently over medium-low heat until slightly thickened.

Cook and drain the pasta, then toss with sauce. (This dish is better if served without grated cheese.)

Penne with Artichoke Ricotta

Yield: 4 servings

3 or 4 slices bacon, chopped
6 Tb butter
3 small artichokes
salt and pepper
⅓ to ½ cup chicken broth
1 cup ricotta cheese
1 lb penne (or mostaccioli)
2 eggs
3 Tb grated Parmesan cheese

In a skillet, sauté bacon in 3 tablespoons of butter. Trim off all but the tenderest parts of the artichokes, and discard the choke. Slice thin, and stir in with bacon. Add salt and pepper to taste, then cook over medium heat, basting occasionally with enough broth to keep from sticking. Cook 15 to 20 minutes, or until artichokes are tender.

In a saucepan, melt remaining 3 tablespoons of butter. Sieve the ricotta, and blend in with melted butter. Press cooked artichoke mixture through a food mill and, together with cooking juices, add to the ricotta. Cook for a few minutes to blend flavors well.

Cook the pasta. Meanwhile, beat eggs together with grated Parmesan, and blend in artichoke-ricotta mixture. When cooked al dente, drain the pasta, then toss with the sauce.

Penne with Artichoke Sauce

Yield: 4 servings

5 small artichokes
1 small onion, sliced
¼ cup oil
1 Tb capers
¾ lb tomatoes, diced
salt and pepper
1 Tb chopped parsley
1 lb penne (or mostaccioli)
½ cup grated Parmesan cheese

Remove hard outer leaves and the choke from artichokes. Trim spiny tips from remaining leaves, and slice artichokes thin. Sauté onion in oil over medium heat. Add artichokes, and brown over high heat. Add capers and diced tomatoes, together with salt and pepper to taste. Turn heat to medium and cook 15 to 20 minutes, or until artichokes are tender. Stir in parsley.

Cook the pasta al dente, drain, then toss with sauce and grated Parmesan to serve.

Penne with Ham and Peas

Yield: 4 servings

1 small onion, chopped
3 Tb oil
4 Tb butter
¾ lb freshly shelled peas (or 10-oz pkg frozen)
salt and pepper
rich chicken broth
4 oz cooked ham
1 lb penne (or mostaccioli)
½ cup Gruyère cheese, diced
½ cup grated Parmesan cheese

In a large skillet, sauté onion in oil and 2 tablespoons of butter. Add peas, then salt and pepper to taste. Cook over medium heat, basting occasionally with broth to keep from sticking. Cut ham in strips, and brown in a small skillet with remaining 2 tablespoons of butter. When peas are almost tender, add sautéed ham to the large skillet.

Cook the pasta, and drain it just before it reaches al dente. Add to skillet, then cook for a few minutes over medium-high heat to blend flavors well. Transfer pasta and sauce to a tureen. Add diced Gruyère, sprinkle with grated Parmesan, then toss gently and serve.

Penne with Piquant Mushroom Sauce

Yield: 4 servings

2 garlic cloves, chopped
4 Tb butter
¼ lb bacon, minced
½ lb fresh mushrooms, sliced
1 lb tomatoes, chopped
salt
hot pepper flakes
1 lb penne (or mostaccioli)
pinch of dried basil
½ cup grated Romano cheese
½ cup grated Parmesan cheese

Sauté garlic in butter until golden. Then sauté bacon in garlic-flavored butter. Add mushrooms, and cook over medium heat for 15 minutes. Strain tomatoes through a sieve or food mill, and add to saucepan. Season to taste with salt and hot pepper flakes.

Cover pan and cook over medium heat for another 20 minutes. Meanwhile, cook the pasta. A few minutes before serving, add basil to the sauce. When cooked al dente, drain the pasta, toss with sauce, and sprinkle with grated cheeses.

Perciatelli alla Marinara

Yield: 4 servings

2 garlic cloves, crushed
hot pepper flakes
½ cup oil
1½ lb tomatoes, chopped
salt
1 lb perciatelli (or thick spaghetti)
¼ lb (10–12) black olives, pitted and chopped
1 Tb capers
1 Tb chopped parsley

Sauté garlic and dash of red pepper flakes in oil until garlic is golden. Strain tomatoes through a sieve or food mill, add salt to taste, and stir into pan mixture. Cook for at least 15 minutes.

Cook the pasta al dente. A few minutes before sauce is done, stir in olives and capers. Drain the pasta, toss with sauce, and sprinkle with chopped parsley to serve. (Cheese is not recommended to accompany this pasta dish.)

Bachelor's Delight Perciatelli

Yield: 4 servings

¾ lb onions
½ cup oil
salt and pepper
dry white wine
1 lb perciatelli (or bucatini)
4 Tb butter, softened
½ cup grated Parmesan cheese

Peel onions and blanch for a few minutes in boiling water; drain, dry, and slice them. Sauté onions in oil. Season with salt and pepper to taste. Baste from time to time with a spoonful of dry white wine. Cook onions to a thick purée. Cook the pasta al dente. Drain and toss with onion sauce, butter, and grated Parmesan. Before serving, let stand for a moment to blend flavors well.

Perciatelli with Bacon and Tomato Sauce

Yield: 4 servings

1 lb perciatelli (or bucatini)
¼ lb lean salt pork (or bacon)
2 Tb oil
1 small onion, chopped
1½ lb tomatoes, chopped
hot pepper flakes
salt
grated Romano cheese

Cook the pasta. Meanwhile, dice salt pork or bacon, and fry in 1 tablespoon of oil until crisp. Drain on paper towels and reserve. Add remaining tablespoon of oil to pan, and sauté onion until tender. Add tomatoes, then hot pepper flakes and salt to taste. Cook for 5 minutes; stir in salt pork. When pasta is cooked al dente, drain and toss with sauce and grated cheese.

Perciatelli with Mussels (p. 42)

Perciatelli Calabrese Style (p. 42)

Perciatelli with Cabbage, Sausage, and Potato

Yield: 4 servings

1 potato, peeled and sliced thin
1 small cabbage, shredded
1 lb perciatelli (or bucatini)
1 small onion, sliced thin
1 Tb butter
1 Tb oil
¼ lb sausage
salt and pepper
½ cup dry white wine
½ cup grated Romano cheese

Cook sliced potato and shredded cabbage in lightly salted boiling water. After a few minutes, break macaroni into short lengths and add to the boiling vegetable pot. While pasta is cooking, sauté onion lightly in butter and oil. Cut sausage in small pieces, add to onion, and continue cooking until sausage is browned. Add salt, pepper, and wine, then cook until wine has evaporated.

When pasta is cooked al dente, drain pasta and vegetables. Place on a serving platter, sprinkle with grated cheese, and toss with sausage and onion sauce.

Perciatelli Calabrese Style

Yield: 4 servings

1 Tb raisins
1 lb fresh sardines (or small smelts)
2 garlic cloves, slightly mashed
½ cup oil
salt
2 Tb bread crumbs

Soak raisins in cold water. Clean sardines and poach; drain when half-cooked. Sauté garlic in oil until golden. Discard garlic, add the fish, and sauté briefly. Add salt, raisins, and bread crumbs, then continue cooking until fish is tender. Cook al dente and drain pasta, then toss gently with sardine sauce.

Perciatelli with Mussels

Yield: 4 servings

3 doz fresh mussels (or clams)
5 Tb oil
4 Tb butter
¼ lb (10–12) black olives, pitted
2 tsp anchovy paste
1 lb tomatoes, chopped
1 garlic clove, chopped
chopped parsley
1 lb perciatelli (or bucatini)

Clean mussels with a stiff brush, then put them in a skillet with oil. Set over medium-high heat until their shells open. Remove mussels from their shells and put them in a bowl. Strain the cooking liquid into the bowl. Heat 2 tablespoons of butter, and sauté the olives together with anchovy paste. Add tomatoes and a few spoons of cooking liquid, then simmer over medium heat to thicken the sauce. Add garlic and parsley to sauce, together with the mussels. Simmer very briefly. Cook pasta al dente, drain, and toss with remaining butter and half the sauce. Serve the rest at table in a sauceboat.

Perciatelli with Ricotta

Yield: 4 servings

1 lb perciatelli (or bucatini)
1 cup ricotta cheese
4 Tb butter, softened
1 tsp cinnamon
1 tsp sugar

Cook the pasta. Meanwhile, put ricotta in a mixing bowl, then add butter, cinnamon, and sugar. Mix with a wooden spoon for several minutes to blend smoothly. Thin the sauce with a little water from the pasta. When pasta is cooked al dente, drain and toss with sauce.

Perciatelli alla Siciliana

Yield: 4 servings

¾ oz (¾ cup) dried mushrooms
1 large eggplant
salt
2 small pork sausages
oil
5 Tb butter
all-purpose flour
1 lb perciatelli (or bucatini)
1 garlic clove, crushed
pinch of sage
1 lb tomatoes, chopped
pepper
grated Parmesan cheese

Soak mushrooms in warm water until spongy, drain, and chop. Slice eggplant in rounds (or cubes), salt lightly, and set on a rack to drain. Peel sausages, dice, and sauté in greased skillet until brown; remove to a plate and set aside. Add 1 tablespoon each of oil and butter to the skillet, and sauté mushrooms. Dry eggplant, dredge in flour, and fry in about ⅛ inch of oil.

Cook pasta. Meanwhile, in a saucepan, sauté garlic in 2 tablespoons of butter with sage. Strain tomatoes through a sieve or food mill, and add to the pan. Season with salt and pepper, and cook for 15 minutes. Add sausage and mushrooms. Warm over low heat to combine flavors. Drain pasta and toss with remaining 2 tablespoons of butter and half the sauce. Arrange eggplant on top, and sprinkle with grated Parmesan. Serve the rest of the sauce at the table.

Perciatelli with Squid

Yield: 4 servings

¾ lb squid
1 lb tomatoes, chopped
2 garlic cloves, minced
½ cup oil
salt and pepper
½ cup dry white wine
2 anchovy fillets, minced
1 lb perciatelli (or bucatini)
1 Tb chopped parsley

Clean the squid, being careful to remove the ink sac. Cut into narrow strips. Strain tomatoes through a sieve or food mill. Sauté garlic in oil until golden. Add squid to the pan, season to taste with salt and pepper, and cook 2 or 3 minutes. Sprinkle with wine. When it has evaporated, add anchovies and tomatoes. Simmer sauce for about 30 minutes, diluting if necessary with a few spoonfuls of warm water. Cook the pasta al dente, drain, and toss with sauce and parsley.

Rigatoni all'Italiana

Yield: 4 servings

2 oz salt pork, chopped fine
6 Tb butter
1 small onion, chopped fine
2 thin slices prosciutto (or baked ham), chopped
¼ lb fresh mushrooms, sliced
¼ lb chicken livers, chopped
½ cup dry red wine
1 lb tomatoes, chopped
salt and pepper
1 lb rigatoni
½ cup grated Parmesan cheese
fresh basil (or parsley), chopped

Sauté salt pork in 3 tablespoons of butter until golden. Add onion, and sauté until transparent. Stir in prosciutto and mushrooms. Add chicken livers and wine, blending well, and continue cooking until wine evaporates. Strain tomatoes through a sieve or a food mill, and add to the saucepan. Season to taste with salt and pepper, then simmer over medium heat for 30 minutes.

Cook the pasta al dente and drain. Sprinkle with grated Parmesan, and toss with sauce and remaining 3 tablespoons of butter. Sprinkle with chopped basil (or parsley) and serve.

Rigatoni with Butternut Squash

Yield: 4 servings

2 lb butternut squash
oil
6 Tb butter
1 lb rigatoni
½ cup grated Parmesan cheese
pinch of nutmeg, freshly grated

Peel and dice squash. Sauté in oil and 4 tablespoons of butter until well browned.

Cook and drain the pasta, then toss with remaining 2 tablespoons of butter and grated Parmesan. Pour sautéed squash over pasta, season lightly with nutmeg, and toss gently to serve.

Rigatoni with Mushroom Sauce

Yield: 4 servings

1 lb rigatoni
½ oz (½ cup) dried mushrooms
4 Tb oil
1 garlic clove, minced
8 anchovy fillets, mashed
1 Tb bread crumbs
1 Tb butter
salt and pepper (optional)

Cook the pasta. Meanwhile, soak dried mushrooms in warm water for 30 minutes, or until they become spongy. Drain, squeeze dry, and chop. Heat oil in a skillet, and sauté garlic until golden. Add mushrooms, blend in mashed anchovies and bread crumbs. Cook over high heat for a few minutes to blend flavors well.

Drain rigatoni, and put them on a serving platter; toss first with butter, then with mushroom sauce to serve. Adjust seasoning to taste with salt and pepper if desired.

Rigatoni with Butternut Squash (p. 44)

Rigatoni with Sausage and Tomato Sauce

Yield: 4 servings

1 small onion, chopped
1 small carrot, chopped
1 bay leaf
4 Tb butter
½ lb sausage
¾ lb tomatoes, chopped
salt and pepper
meat broth
1 lb rigatoni
1 Tb marjoram
¾ cup grated Parmesan cheese

Sauté onion, carrot, and bay leaf in butter. Skin sausage, break stuffing in pieces, add to the saucepan, and sauté until well browned. Strain tomatoes through a sieve or food mill, and add to the pan. Season to taste with salt and pepper, then simmer gently over medium heat, basting occasionally with just enough broth to make a thick sauce.

Cook the pasta. When sauce has thickened, add marjoram and remove from heat. Drain pasta, sprinkle with grated Parmesan, and toss with meat sauce.

Shells with Leafy Greens

Yield: 4 servings

2 lb broccoli rabe*
salt
1 lb large pasta shells (e.g., orecchiette)
1 garlic clove, chopped
4 anchovy fillets, minced
oil

*Mustard or turnip greens, Swiss chard, or spinach may also be used in preparing this dish.

Wash greens in several changes of water. Separate the blossoms, leaves, and stems, keeping all three. Chop stems and, together with leaves, put them in 4 quarts of lightly salted boiling water. After a few minutes, add pasta; then, about halfway through the cooking, add the blossoms. Sauté garlic and anchovy fillets in a large skillet with a generous amount of oil. Drain pasta and greens while pasta is still firm, then transfer to the skillet. Continue mixing pasta and sauce over low heat for a few minutes; serve in a tureen. (No cheese is recommended to accompany this dish.)

Shells with Meat Sauce

Yield: 4 servings

1 carrot
1 small onion
1 stalk celery
4 or 5 sprigs parsley
2 Tb butter
2 Tb oil
1 bay leaf
½ lb ground beef
½ lb bulk sausage stuffing (or link sausages, sliced)
¼ cup dry red wine
salt and pepper
1¼ lb tomatoes, chopped
1 lb large pasta shells (e.g., orecchiette)
½ cup grated Parmesan cheese

Chop carrot, onion, and celery together with parsley, and sauté them in butter and oil. When onion is wilted, add bay leaf, ground beef, and sausage. Sauté briefly. Stir in wine, then continue cooking until wine evaporates. Season to taste with salt and pepper. Strain tomatoes through a sieve or food mill; add them to the saucepan, and simmer gently for at least 1 hour. Remove bay leaf from sauce. Cook and drain the pasta. Toss it with meat sauce, and sprinkle with grated Parmesan to serve.

Shells with Peas and Bacon

Yield: 4 servings

1 thick slice fat smoked bacon
1 thick slice fat unsmoked bacon (or salt pork)
1 Tb butter
1 Tb oil
1½ lb tomatoes, chopped
½ lb freshly shelled peas (or 10-oz pkg frozen)*
salt and pepper
pinch of oregano
1 lb large pasta shells (e.g., cavatelli)

Dice the two kinds of bacon, then sauté in butter and oil until golden brown. Add tomatoes to the pan, together with peas. Add salt and pepper to taste, cover, and simmer gently over medium heat for 5 minutes. Add oregano, and cook for about 5 more minutes, or until peas are tender but not mushy. Cook the pasta al dente, drain, and toss with sauce. (Do not use grated cheese with this dish.)

*Canned peas may also be used: drain liquid and add peas only when other ingredients are well cooked.

Shells with Provolone

Yield: 4 servings

1 lb large pasta shells (e.g., cavatelli)
1-lb wedge provolone cheese
¼ lb butter
black pepper, freshly ground

Cook the pasta, drain, and reserve about ¼ cup of the boiled water. While pasta is cooking, grate half the provolone, and cut the other half in very thin slices. Cut butter into small dabs, and toss with the pasta. Mix grated cheese with reserved cooking water, and stir this paste in with the pasta. Season generously with fresh ground pepper. Toss with the finely sliced cheese and serve.

Spaghetti with Garlic and Oil

Yield: 4 servings

1 lb spaghetti
½ cup olive oil
2 garlic cloves, minced
hot pepper flakes
2 Tb butter, softened

Cook the spaghetti al dente. A few minutes before draining the pasta, heat olive oil in a small saucepan. Add garlic and hot pepper flakes to taste, then sauté until garlic is golden. (Do not allow it to brown.)

Drain spaghetti and transfer to a warm bowl. Toss quickly with garlic sauce, which should be very hot, and butter. Serve immediately.

Spaghetti Buccaneer Style

Yield: 4 servings

2 garlic cloves, crushed
4 Tb oil
hot pepper flakes
black pepper, freshly ground
1 lb tomatoes, chopped
salt
1½ doz clams (or 6½-oz can minced)
¼ lb squid
¼ lb shelled shrimp
1 lb spaghetti
chopped parsley

In a skillet, sauté crushed garlic in 2 tablespoons of oil with a few hot pepper flakes and a pinch of fresh ground black pepper. Add tomatoes and salt to taste, then simmer for about 15 minutes over medium heat.

If fresh clams are used, steam open first in a large saucepot, and set aside to cool. Clean and dice squid and shrimp, and sauté in remaining 2 tablespoons of oil in a saucepan. When they are almost tender, add tomato sauce and minced clams, then cook for a few minutes, or until squid is tender. Turn off heat.

Cook the spaghetti al dente, drain, and toss with hot seafood sauce. Sprinkle with chopped parsley and serve. (As with other seafood sauces, cheese is not recommended in serving.)

Spaghetti Shepherd Style

Yield: 4 servings

1 lb spaghetti (or long thin macaroni)
½ lb ricotta cheese
6 Tb butter, softened
salt
hot pepper flakes

If using long macaroni, break it into short pieces before cooking. While pasta is cooking, mix a little of the boiling water with ricotta, butter, salt, and a few hot pepper flakes to make a smooth sauce. When cooked al dente, drain the pasta, and toss with spiced ricotta sauce to serve.

Piquant Noodles with Fresh Tomatoes (p. 35)

Spicy Spaghetti alla Calabrese

Yield: 4 servings

1 lb spaghetti
1 garlic clove, minced
½ cup oil
hot pepper flakes
2 oz anchovy fillets
1 Tb chopped parsley
salt (optional)

Cook the pasta. While it is cooking, sauté garlic in oil until golden. Add a few hot pepper flakes. Mash anchovies with a fork, then stir into the pan along with chopped parsley. Drain spaghetti, and toss with anchovy-pepper sauce. Add a pinch of salt to taste, if necessary.

Spaghetti alla Carbonara

Yield: 4 servings

4 eggs
salt
black pepper, freshly ground
1 or 2 Tb heavy cream
½ cup grated Parmesan (or Romano) cheese
  (or ¼ cup of each)
¼ lb bacon, diced
2 Tb butter
1 Tb oil
1 lb spaghetti

Beat eggs in a large serving bowl. Add salt and pepper to taste, heavy cream, and grated cheese. Sauté bacon in butter and oil.

Cook the spaghetti al dente, drain and add to the egg mixture. Toss with a wooden spoon and fork, lifting the spaghetti thoroughly to blend the mixture well. Pour sautéed bacon and pan juices over the pasta, toss, and serve with additional grated cheese and the pepper mill at the table.

Spaghetti Deliziosi

Yield: 4 servings

1 large eggplant
salt
4 Tb butter
½ small onion, chopped
1 garlic clove, minced
½ chicken breast, cooked and diced
1 thick slice prosciutto (or baked ham), diced
black pepper, freshly ground
2 Tb brandy (optional)
¾ lb tomatoes, chopped
oil
1 lb spaghetti
½ cup grated Parmesan cheese
6 thin slices mozzarella cheese

Cut eggplant in thin slices, sprinkle with salt, and set on a rack to drain. Melt 2 tablespoons of butter in a saucepan, and sauté onion and garlic until golden. Add diced chicken and prosciutto. Season with fresh ground pepper and cook briefly, stirring with a wooden spoon. Add brandy, then cook over medium heat until it evaporates. Stir in tomatoes and simmer for 10 minutes. Dry the eggplant with paper towels, and fry in enough oil to come about ⅛ inch up the sides of the skillet.

Cook and drain pasta, and toss with remaining 2 tablespoons of butter and the grated Parmesan. Top with slices of mozzarella, pour over half the tomato sauce, and arrange slices of sautéed eggplant on top. Put remaining sauce in a sauceboat for individual service at table.

Spaghetti with Four Cheeses

2 oz Swiss cheese   Yield: 4 servings
2 oz fontina cheese
2 oz Gouda cheese
½ cup grated Parmesan cheese
1 lb spaghetti
4 Tb butter, softened
black pepper, freshly ground

Slice the first three cheeses as thin as possible, and put them in a soup tureen. Sprinkle with grated Parmesan. Cook the pasta al dente, drain, and transfer immediately to tureen. Add butter and pepper to taste, mixing thoroughly with a wooden spoon. (The cheeses underneath should melt nicely if the pasta is hot enough when tossed.)

Four-Flavor Spaghetti

Yield: 4 servings

1 whole cooked chicken breast
2 oz spiced tongue
1 black truffle (optional)
2 oz Gruyère (or Swiss) cheese
1 lb spaghetti
½ cup grated Parmesan cheese
1 cup heavy cream
4 Tb butter
black pepper, freshly ground

Skin the chicken breast. Cut chicken, tongue, and truffle in thin strips. Slice the Gruyère (or Swiss) in strips as thin as possible.

Cook the spaghetti. When pasta is half-cooked, ladle about ¼ cup of boiling water from the kettle into a small saucepan. Add grated Parmesan, cream, and butter to hot water, then bring to a simmer. (Do not allow sauce to boil.)

Preheat oven to 400°. Drain the pasta, and toss in a heatproof dish together with sauce. Cover with strips of chicken breast, tongue, truffle, and Gruyère. Place dish in the hot oven and turn off heat. Serve as soon as cheese is melted.

Spaghetti with Mushrooms, Anchovies, and Peppers

Yield: 4 servings

¼ oz (¼ cup) dried mushrooms
2 garlic cloves, crushed
4 anchovy fillets, minced
3 Tb oil
1 bay leaf
1 sweet pepper, minced
1 lb tomatoes, chopped
2 Tb chopped parsley
1 Tb capers, chopped
pinch of oregano
black pepper, freshly ground
1 lb spaghetti

Soak dried mushrooms in warm water; drain and mince. Mash garlic together with anchovies, and sauté in oil until garlic is golden. Add bay leaf, sweet pepper, mushrooms, and tomatoes and mix well. Then stir in parsley, capers, and a good pinch of oregano. Season with fresh ground black pepper, and add salt if necessary. Continue cooking over medium heat for another 30 minutes.

Cook the spaghetti al dente, drain, and toss with sauce. (This pasta dish is best when served without grated cheese. For those who insist, however, pecorino, Romano, or some other rather sharp grated cheese is recommended.)

Spaghetti with Mussels and Mushrooms

Yield: 4 servings

¾ oz (¾ cup) dried mushrooms
2 doz mussels
½ small onion, chopped
2 Tb butter
1 Tb oil
¾ lb tomatoes, chopped
salt and pepper
1 lb spaghetti

Soak mushrooms in warm water until they become spongy. Scrub mussels, put them in a large saucepan with a bottom cover of water or white wine, then cover with lid and set over high heat until they open. Discard shells, and place mussels in an earthenware dish. Strain cooking liquid and add to mussels.

Sauté onion in butter and oil until transparent. Stir in tomatoes, and season to taste with salt and pepper. Drain and slice mushrooms, and add to the sauce. Simmer until mushrooms are tender.

Meanwhile cook and drain spaghetti. A few minutes before removing the sauce from heat, add mussels and their broth. Toss pasta in the sauce.

Spaghetti Papal Style

Yield: 4 servings

1 lb spaghetti
½ cup olive oil
8 slices lean bacon, diced
4 eggs
½ cup grated Parmesan
salt and pepper

Cook the pasta. Meanwhile, heat olive oil in a large skillet,* and sauté bacon over medium heat. Beat eggs together with grated Parmesan and salt and pepper to taste. Drain the spaghetti when barely tender, and add to bacon in the skillet; then pour the beaten egg mixture over pasta. Mix quickly and remove from heat as soon as egg begins thickening. Serve immediately.

*In Italy, this dish is traditionally cooked and served in an earthenware skillet.

Spaghetti alla Puttanesca

Yield: 4 servings

2 garlic cloves, minced
4 anchovy fillets, minced
2 Tb oil
6 oz (about 20) black olives, pitted and sliced
1 Tb capers, chopped
1¼ lb tomatoes, chopped
hot pepper flakes (optional)
1 lb spaghetti
1 Tb chopped parsley

Sauté garlic and anchovies in oil. When garlic is golden (but not browned), add olives, capers, tomatoes, and a few hot pepper flakes. Simmer for about 15 minutes.

Cook and drain the pasta, toss with sauce, then garnish with chopped parsley to serve.

Spaghetti with Mussels and Mushrooms (p. 52)

Spicy Spaghetti alla Calabrese (p. 50)

Spaghetti San Giovannino

Yield: 4 servings

3 Tb chopped fresh basil
1 garlic clove, minced
4 anchovy fillets, minced
½ cup oil
¾ lb tomatoes, chopped
2 Tb chicken broth (or fish stock)
salt and pepper
1 lb spaghetti
1 Tb capers

Sauté basil, garlic, and anchovies in oil. Strain tomatoes through a food mill and add to the pan, together with broth. Season to taste with salt and pepper. Cook sauce over medium-high heat for about 5 minutes, stirring with a wooden spoon. Add capers, and cook for another minute or two.

Cook and drain spaghetti, then toss with sauce to serve.

Cold Spaghetti with Tuna

Yield: 4 servings

1 lb spaghetti
7 oz chunk tuna in oil
½ cup olive oil
lemon juice
pinch of oregano
black pepper, freshly ground
1 Tb capers

Cook and drain the spaghetti, then rinse quickly under cold running water to cool. Shred tuna with a fork, dress with olive oil and a few drops of lemon juice, and pour mixture over the spaghetti. Sprinkle with oregano, fresh ground pepper, and capers, and toss gently.

Spaghetti with Tuna Sauce

Yield: 4 servings

2 garlic cloves, minced
4 Tb oil
1¼ lb tomatoes, chopped
salt and pepper
3 or 4 anchovy fillets
4 Tb butter, softened
7 oz chunk tuna in oil
1 lb spaghetti
fresh parsley, chopped

Sauté garlic in 2 tablespoons of oil. Stir in tomatoes and salt and pepper to taste. Simmer over low heat until sauce thickens.

Mash anchovy fillets in a bowl with a fork. Blend in butter, and mix to a smooth, creamy consistency. Heat remaining 2 tablespoons of oil, and sauté tuna until lightly browned. Stir in tomato sauce, add the anchovy butter, then cook over low heat to blend flavors well.

Cook and drain pasta, toss with sauce, and sprinkle with chopped parsley to serve.

Spaghetti with Tuna, Bacon, and Mushrooms

Yield: 4 servings

1 garlic clove, slightly mashed
2 Tb oil
½ lb fresh mushrooms, sliced
3 or 4 slices bacon, diced
salt and pepper
3 oz chunk tuna
1 lb spaghetti
1 or 2 Tb beef drippings (optional)
grated Parmesan cheese

Sauté garlic in oil until golden, then discard. Sauté mushrooms and bacon in garlic-flavored oil. Add salt and pepper to taste, then continue cooking over medium heat. Just before mushrooms are fully cooked, shred tuna and add to the saucepan. Cook until mushrooms are tender.

Cook and drain spaghetti. Pour on beef drippings and the mushroom-tuna mixture. Grated Parmesan may be served at table for a light garnish, to individual taste.

Spaghetti Turiddu

Yield: 4 servings

½ cup oil
2 garlic cloves, minced
black pepper, freshly ground
4 anchovy fillets, minced
2 small sweet pickles, chopped
1 Tb capers
6 or 8 black olives, pitted and sliced
1 lb tomatoes, chopped
salt
1 lb spaghetti
1 Tb chopped fresh basil
pinch of oregano

Heat oil and sauté garlic until golden, seasoning to taste with fresh ground pepper. Stir in anchovies, pickles, capers, olives, and tomatoes. Add salt to taste, then simmer over medium-high heat for 15 minutes.

Cook and drain the pasta, toss with sauce, and sprinkle with chopped basil and oregano to serve.

Spaghetti with Walnut Sauce

Yield: 4 servings

1 cup shelled walnuts
1 Tb pine nuts
4 Tb butter (or oil)
½ cup grated Parmesan cheese
2 garlic cloves, chopped
1 tsp olive oil
salt and pepper
1 lb spaghetti

Toast shelled walnuts lightly in preheated 400° oven, then remove the outer skin. Crush walnuts and pine nuts with a mortar and pestle (or else in a blender or food processor). When they are ground quite fine, heat butter and sauté nut meal briefly. Press through a sieve into a bowl, and add grated Parmesan and chopped garlic. Add teaspoon of olive oil and enough hot water to make a fairly thick sauce. Season to taste with salt and pepper, and blend well.

Cook and drain spaghetti, then toss with walnut sauce. Additional grated Parmesan may be served at table.

Spaghetti with Zucchini

Yield: 4 servings

1 lb spaghetti
1 lb zucchini
2 Tb oil
1 garlic clove, crushed
salt and pepper
2 Tb grated Parmesan cheese

Cook the pasta. Meanwhile, wash and trim off the ends of the zucchini, then parboil by cooking for 10 minutes in lightly salted boiling water. Drain, slice, and sauté zucchini briefly in a skillet with oil and garlic. Season to taste with salt and pepper.

When cooked al dente, drain spaghetti, toss with sautéed zucchini, then sprinkle with grated Parmesan and serve.

Vermicelli with Mushrooms

Yield: 4 servings

1 garlic clove, chopped
fresh parsley, chopped
2 Tb oil
4 Tb butter
12 oz fresh mushrooms, sliced
salt and pepper
1 lb tomatoes, chopped
1 lb vermicelli (or thin spaghetti)

Sauté garlic and parsley in oil and 2 tablespoons of butter. Add sliced mushrooms, and cook for about 5 minutes. Add salt and pepper to taste, then stir in tomatoes. Bring to a boil, reduce heat, and simmer until mushrooms are very tender.

Cook and drain the pasta, then toss with remaining 2 tablespoons of butter and mushroom sauce.

Vermicelli with Saffron

Yield: 4 servings

pinch of saffron
1 cup heavy cream
¼ lb cooked ham (in 1 piece), diced
½ cup grated Parmesan cheese
2 egg yolks
salt
1 lb vermicelli (or thin spaghetti)
1 hard-cooked egg yolk
fresh parsley, chopped

In a saucepan, crumble and dissolve saffron in a few tablespoons of warm water. Add heavy cream, ham, and grated Parmesan. Bring almost to a boil, then remove from heat. Cool slightly and add egg yolks, stirring briskly with a whisk to blend. Season to taste with salt, and keep warm. Cook and drain the pasta, then toss with cream sauce. Push hard-cooked egg yolk through a sieve (or crumble finely), and sprinkle over the pasta. Garnish with chopped parsley to serve.

Fettuccine alla Bolognese (p. 22)

Vermicelli with Venetian Walnut Sauce

Yield: 4 servings

1 lb vermicelli
1 cup shelled walnuts
¼ tsp sugar
¼ tsp cinnamon
nutmeg, freshly grated
salt and pepper
¼ cup oil
2 Tb bread crumbs
1½ Tb butter

Cook vermicelli al dente. While pasta is cooking, mash walnuts in a mortar. Transfer to a mixing bowl, and then add sugar, cinnamon, nutmeg, and salt and pepper to taste. Add oil and 1 or 2 tablespoons of boiling water from pasta pot.

Sauté bread crumbs in butter. Drain vermicelli, and toss gently with walnut sauce. Sprinkle with sautéed bread crumbs and serve. (Do not use any grated cheese with this dish.)

Ziti with Eggplant Sicilian Style

Yield: 4 servings

2 small eggplants, diced
salt
1 sweet yellow or red pepper
3 Tb oil
3 anchovy fillets, chopped
pinch of basil
¼ lb (10–12) black olives, pitted
1 Tb capers
1½ lb tomatoes, chopped
pepper
1 lb ziti (or rigatoni)

Sprinkle eggplant with salt and set in a colander to drain. Roast the pepper by holding it with a long-handled fork directly over high heat on a gas or electric burner. Turn pepper frequently until skin becomes blackened and blistered. Under cold running water, peel off burnt skin. Core and seed the pepper, and cut in strips.

Heat oil in a skillet. Dry eggplant with paper towels and add to the pan, together with pepper strips, anchovies, basil, olives, and capers. Cook briefly to blend flavors well. Strain tomatoes through a sieve or food mill, and add to the pan. Season to taste with salt and pepper. Cover and simmer, stirring occasionally, for about 30 minutes, or until sauce is smooth and somewhat thickened. Cook pasta al dente, drain, and toss with sauce.

Ziti with Gorgonzola

Yield: 4 servings

1 lb ziti (or rigatoni)
½ cup heavy cream
7 Tb butter
salt and pepper
¼ lb mild gorgonzola (or other blue cheese)
chopped parsley

Cook the pasta. Meanwhile, warm cream and butter together over medium heat. Season lightly with salt and pepper, and when cream sauce begins simmering, remove from heat. Dice gorgonzola in small pieces. When pasta is cooked al dente, drain and toss with gorgonzola bits and cream sauce. Mix well, then garnish with chopped parsley to serve.

Ziti with Pork Ragout Sauce

Yield: 4 servings

1 lb ziti (or rigatoni)
3 or 4 slices bacon
2 Tb oil
Pork Ragout Sauce (see Index)
chopped parsley
½ cup grated Parmesan cheese

Cook and drain the pasta. Meanwhile, broil or fry bacon until very crisp. Toss pasta with oil and hot ragout sauce, then garnish with crumbled bacon bits and chopped parsley. Serve accompanied with grated Parmesan at the table.

Ziti South Italian Style

Yield: 4 servings

1 Tb raisins
4 Tb lard
1 small onion, minced
1 garlic clove, minced
2 slices bacon, diced
¾ lb ground beef
½ cup dry white wine
1 lb tomatoes, chopped
1 lb ziti (or rigatoni)
2 Tb oil
black pepper, freshly ground
grated Romano cheese

Soak raisins in a little water. In a large saucepan, melt lard and sauté onion, garlic, and bacon. Add the ground beef, and cook until meat is no longer pink. Stir in the wine, simmering over medium-high heat until it evaporates. Drain raisins and add them, along with tomatoes, to saucepan. Reduce to low heat and simmer the sauce, stirring occasionally, for 1 hour.

Cook and drain the pasta. Toss with oil and half the sauce. Season with a few turns of freshly ground black pepper, and sprinkle generously with grated Romano cheese. Put remainder of the sauce in a sauceboat for individual service at table.

Ziti with Tuna Sauce

Yield: 4 servings

1 small onion, minced
1 garlic clove, minced
2 Tb oil
4 anchovy fillets
1 lb tomatoes, chopped
pinch of oregano
salt and pepper
3¼ oz chunk tuna in oil
1 lb ziti (or rigatoni)
½ cup grated Romano cheese

Sauté onion and garlic in oil. Mash anchovy fillets thoroughly with a fork, and add to the saucepan. Strain tomatoes through a food mill or sieve, then add to sauce. Stir in oregano and salt and pepper to taste. Bring to a boil, reduce heat, and simmer for about 20 minutes. Flake the tuna with a fork, and add to sauce.

Cook and drain the pasta. Toss with tuna sauce, and sprinkle with grated Romano cheese.

Oven-Baked and Stuffed Pastas

STUFFED PASTA

Stuffed pasta is made in a variety of shapes and sizes bearing names such as cannelloni, cappelletti, ravioli, agnolotti, and tortellini, to name some of the more familiar. All forms have a meat, cheese, or vegetable filling. Given here are directions for preparing two of the most popular types, cappelletti and ravioli.

Cappelletti (the Italian word means "little hats"): Use a cutting wheel to make little squares. Spread each square with a bit of filling, then fold over on the diagonal to make into triangles. Seal by pressing the edges together with your fingers. Twist the two base corners of the triangle around your index finger and join them by squeezing the corners together (see illustrations on p. 13).

Ravioli: Distribute the filling over half the sheet of dough in small, equally spaced mounds about 2 inches apart. Fold the empty half of the sheet over the filled, and set it down gently to cover the mounds. Carefully press the top layer of dough against the lower one in the spaces between mounds. Cut out the individual ravioli with a pastry wheel, cutting in straight lines first in one direction, then at right angles to form small filled squares.

For round ravioli, cut the dough in small circles using a special circular punch (sold in specialty cookware shops) or a deep biscuit cutter. You may also place the rim of a downturned water glass on top of the filled dough and cut around its edge with a pastry wheel, or else use the rim itself as a cutting edge by carefully applying sufficient force with a rotary motion.

Baked Noodles alla Siciliana (p. 70)

Cannelloni Lazio Style

Yield: 4 servings

Basic Pasta Dough (see Index)

For the filling:
½ oz (½ cup) dried mushrooms
½ small onion, chopped
1 carrot, chopped
1 stalk celery, chopped
4 Tb butter
2 oz prosciutto (or baked ham), diced
¾ lb ground beef
½ lb ground veal
salt and pepper
pinch of nutmeg, freshly grated
½ cup dry white wine
1 tsp all-purpose flour
1 lb tomatoes, chopped

For the sauce and baking:
Bolognese Meat Sauce (see Index)
4 Tb butter, softened
1 cup grated Parmesan cheese

Prepare pasta dough as directed, but with only 2 cups of flour. Cut dough in rectangles about 3 by 4 inches.

For the filling: Soak the mushrooms in warm water until spongy, drain, and slice. Sauté onion, carrot, and celery in butter. Add prosciutto, ground beef and veal, and mushrooms. Sauté until the meat is well browned. Season to taste with salt, pepper, and nutmeg. Add wine and flour. Strain the tomatoes through a food mill or sieve, then add to sauce. Bring to a boil, reduce heat, and simmer until sauce thickens. Let stand to cool.

Cook the pasta rectangles, a few at a time, and drain while still slightly underdone. Set out to cool on a dry dish towel. Spread the filling on the pasta rectangles, then roll loosely along the long side to form canelloni. Preheat oven to 400°. Butter a shallow ovenproof dish, and arrange cannelloni in one or two layers. Top each layer with sauce, dab with butter, and sprinkle with grated Parmesan. Bake for 15 minutes, or until lightly browned.

Cannelloni with Spinach and Meat

Yield: 4 servings

Basic Pasta Dough (see Index)

For the filling:
1½ lb fresh spinach (or 2 10-oz pkg frozen)
3 Tb butter
3 Tb tomato sauce
¾ cup grated Parmesan cheese
2 hard-cooked egg yolks
pinch of salt
¼ lb roast veal, ground
¼ lb roast pork, ground
¼ lb cooked beef tongue, ground

Prepare pasta dough as directed, but with only 2 cups of flour. Cut dough in rectangles about 3 by 4 inches.

For the filling: Cook spinach in lightly salted water, drain, squeeze dry, chop, and sauté briefly in butter. Remove from heat, and add tomato sauce, grated Parmesan, egg yolks, and salt to taste. Stir in the mixed ground meats, then blend all these ingredients thoroughly.

For the sauce: In another pan, melt 6 tablespoons of butter, and blend in flour. Gradually add the milk, stirring constantly, and cook over low heat until sauce becomes thick and smooth. Remove from heat, and season to taste with salt and pepper. Then add 2 tablespoons of cream sauce to the filling, blending well.

▷

For the sauce and baking:
8 Tb butter, softened
5 Tb all-purpose flour
2 cups milk, heated
salt and pepper
1 cup grated Parmesan cheese

Cook the pasta rectangles, a few at a time, and drain while still slightly underdone. Spread the filling on the pasta rectangles, then roll loosely along the long side to form cannelloni. Preheat oven to 400°. Butter a shallow ovenproof serving dish, and arrange cannelloni in one or two layers. Top each layer with cream sauce, dab with remaining butter, and sprinkle with grated Parmesan. Bake pasta for 15 minutes, or until lightly browned.

Cappelletti with Cream Sauce

Yield: 4 servings

Dough for Stuffed Pasta (see Index)

For the filling:
¼ lb ground pork
¼ lb ground veal
2 Tb butter
½ cup grated Parmesan cheese
1 tsp bread crumbs
few sprigs fresh parsley, minced
¼ lb prosciutto (or baked ham), minced
salt and pepper
pinch of nutmeg, freshly ground
1 or 2 Tb meat broth

For the sauce:
5 or 6 fresh sage leaves, crushed
    (or pinch of dried)
4 Tb butter
1 cup heavy cream
salt and pepper
grated Parmesan cheese

Prepare stuffed pasta dough as directed.

For the filling: Sauté ground pork and veal in butter until well browned. Transfer to a mixing bowl, and add grated Parmesan, bread crumbs, parsley, and prosciutto. Season to taste with salt, pepper, and nutmeg. Moisten with broth and mix thoroughly.

Prepare and cook cappelletti according to instructions given in the Introduction to this section.

Meanwhile, prepare the sauce: Warm the sage leaves in butter over low heat. Add heavy cream, and heat until it barely simmers. Do not allow it to boil. Season to taste with salt and pepper. Drain the cappelletti, pour sauce over them, and sprinkle with grated Parmesan cheese to serve.

Cappelletti alla Romagnola

Yield: 4 servings

Dough for Stuffed Pasta (see Index)

For the filling:
½ lb turkey breast
¼ lb lean pork
2 Tb butter
3 or 4 fresh sage leaves, crushed
  (or pinch of dried)
pinch of fresh or dried rosemary, crushed
salt and pepper
½ cup ricotta cheese
⅓ cup grated Parmesan cheese
½ tsp grated lemon peel
2 eggs
pinch of nutmeg, freshly ground

Prepare stuffed pasta dough as directed.

For the filling: Brown the turkey breast and pork in butter with sage and rosemary. Season to taste with salt and pepper. Grind the sautéed meat. Combine in a bowl with ricotta, grated Parmesan, and lemon peel. Bind with 2 eggs. Season to taste with salt, pepper, and nutmeg.

Prepare cappelletti according to instructions given in the Introduction to this section. Cook and drain the cappelletti, pour ragout sauce over them, and sprinkle with grated Parmesan.

For the sauce:
Pork Ragout Sauce (see Index)
½ cup grated Parmesan cheese

Lasagne with Spinach and Ricotta

Yield: 4 servings

Basic Pasta Dough (see Index); or 1 lb lasagne noodles

For the sauce and baking:
½ oz (½ cup) dried mushrooms
2 or 3 slices bacon, chopped
½ small onion, chopped
2 Tb oil
½ lb ground beef
salt and pepper
2 chicken livers, chopped
1 Tb tomato sauce
1½ lb fresh spinach (or 2 10-oz pkg frozen)
½ lb ricotta cheese
¾ cup grated Parmesan cheese
1 egg, beaten lightly
pinch of nutmeg, freshly grated

Prepare pasta dough as directed, but with 4 cups of flour. Cut dough in rectangular strips about 3 by 6 inches.

Soak mushrooms in warm water until spongy. Sauté bacon and onion in oil until onion is transparent. Add ground beef, season to taste with salt and pepper, and cook until beef is well browned. Add chicken livers. Drain and chop mushrooms, then add to the saucepan. Dilute tomato sauce with 2 or 3 tablespoons of water, and stir in. Simmer over medium heat for 15 minutes, adding water or broth occasionally if necessary to keep mixture moist.

Boil and drain spinach, squeeze dry, and chop. Mix with ricotta, half of the grated Parmesan, egg, and salt and nutmeg to taste.

Cook the pasta and drain while still slightly underdone. Then set out to cool on a clean dish towel. Preheat oven to 400°. Butter a rectangular ovenproof dish or baking pan, and fill with alternate layers of lasagne noodles, meat sauce, grated Parmesan, and the spinach-ricotta mixture. Finish with a layer of lasagne, topped with plenty of meat sauce and grated Parmesan. Bake for about 15 minutes, or until lightly browned.

Lasagne Gourmet (p. 66)

Lasagne with Spinach and Ricotta (p. 64)

Lasagne Gourmet

Yield: 4 servings

Basic Pasta Dough *(see Index); or 1 lb lasagne
  noodles*
For the sauce and baking:
½ *lb ground beef*
1 egg
1 Tb chopped parsley
1 garlic clove, chopped
salt and pepper
1 cup all-purpose flour
8 Tb butter
½ cup dry white wine
½ cup meat broth
2 cups milk
¼ lb cooked ham, chopped
1 cup heavy cream
1 lb mozzarella cheese, sliced
1 cup Basic Italian Tomato Sauce (see Index)

Prepare pasta dough as directed, and then cut dough in large rectangles, about 3 by 6 inches. Let dry while preparing the sauce.

In a mixing bowl, combine ground beef, egg, parsley, garlic, and salt and pepper to taste. Form mixture into small meatballs, about 1 inch across. Dredge in flour, and sauté over high heat in 4 tablespoons of butter. Pour in wine and broth, reduce heat, and simmer to thicken sauce.

Prepare a Béchamel Sauce: In a saucepan, melt remaining 4 tablespoons of butter, sift in ½ cup of flour, and mix well. Bring milk nearly to a boil, and add slowly to butter and flour. Cook, stirring constantly, for a few minutes, or until thickened. Remove from heat, and stir in chopped ham and heavy cream.

Cook lasagne, draining while still slightly undercooked, and set out the strips on a clean dish towel to dry. Preheat oven to 400°. Arrange a layer of lasagne in the bottom of a buttered ovenproof dish, square or rectangular. Place several meatballs atop the lasagne, then cover with a little tomato sauce, Béchamel, and a few slices of mozzarella. Add another layer of lasagne, and continue layering as before until you have used all the ingredients, topping off with a layer of Béchamel, tomato sauce, and mozzarella. Bake for about 15 minutes, or until cheese is melted and golden brown.

Spinach Lasagne with Meat Sauce

Yield: 4 servings

*Green Pasta Dough (see Index); or 1 lb green
(spinach) lasagne noodles*

For the sauce:
1 onion, minced
1 carrot, minced
1 stalk celery, minced
8 Tb butter
1¼ lb ground beef
1 tsp all-purpose flour
meat broth
1 Tb minced parsley
½ tsp thyme leaves, crushed
1 bay leaf
pinch of ground clove
salt and pepper
¾ lb chicken giblets, chopped
1 cup grated Parmesan cheese
1 truffle (optional)

Prepare pasta dough as directed. Cut in rectangular strips about 3 by 6 inches.

For the meat sauce: Sauté onion, carrot, and celery in 4 tablespoons of butter. Add ground beef, and sauté over medium heat until browned. Add flour and blend well. Add broth to cover, together with parsley, thyme, bay leaf, and clove. Season to taste with salt and pepper, then cook for 10 minutes. Sauté giblets in 2 tablespoons of butter, and add to the sauce. Cook until giblets are tender. Remove and discard bay leaf.

Preheat oven to 400°. Cook lasagne, and drain while still slightly underdone. Butter an ovenproof dish, and fill with alternate layers of lasagne, meat sauce, grated Parmesan, and grated truffle. Dot the top layer of pasta with butter, and sprinkle generously with grated cheese. Bake for 30 minutes, or until lightly browned.

Macaroni au Gratin

Yield: 4 servings

1 lb large elbow macaroni
2 Tb butter
2 Tb all-purpose flour
1 cup milk, heated
salt and pepper
⅓ cup grated Parmesan cheese

Cook the macaroni al dente. Preheat oven to 350°.

Meanwhile, prepare a Béchamel Sauce: Melt butter in a saucepan, and blend in flour. Stir until smooth. Gradually blend in milk. Bring to a boil, reduce heat, and simmer gently for 5 or 6 minutes, stirring constantly until sauce is smooth and thick. Season to taste with salt and pepper, remove from heat, and set aside to cool.

Drain macaroni while still slightly underdone, then place in a buttered baking dish. Cover with Béchamel Sauce, sprinkle with grated Parmesan, and bake for about 20 minutes, or until a thin golden crust has formed on the surface. Serve immediately, accompanying with additional grated Parmesan and fresh ground pepper at table.

Macaroni Meat Pie with Mushrooms

Yield: 6 servings

For the pie crust:
3 cups all-purpose flour
¾ cup butter
1 egg
1 tsp salt

For the filling:
1 small onion, chopped
1 small carrot, chopped
6 Tb butter
¾ lb beef, diced
½ lb chicken livers and gizzards, sliced thin
¼ lb fresh mushrooms, sliced thin
½ cup dry white wine
1 lb tomatoes, chopped
pinch of thyme leaves, crushed
1 small bay leaf, crumbled
salt and pepper
beef broth
¾ lb large elbow macaroni
½ cup grated Parmesan cheese

For the pie crust: Mix flour, butter, egg, and salt, then knead until smooth. Wrap dough in a dish towel and refrigerate.

For the filling: Sauté chopped onion and carrot in 4 tablespoons of butter until tender. Add diced beef, and sauté until brown. Add chicken livers and gizzards, then mushroom slices, and sauté together briefly. Stir in wine, and simmer until wine evaporates. Press tomatoes through a sieve or food mill, and add to the saucepan along with thyme and bay leaf. Season to taste with salt and pepper. Add 1 or 2 tablespoons or beef broth, and cook for another 30 minutes.

Preheat oven to 375°. Cook elbow macaroni, and drain while still slightly underdone. Toss with remaining 2 tablespoons of butter, half the meat sauce, and grated Parmesan. Butter a deep ovenproof dish or pie pan. Roll out the dough, and use three-quarters of it to line the baking dish. Fill with the pasta. Roll out remaining dough into a circle the diameter of the baking dish or pie pan, and cover the pasta filling with this, pinching the edges together to seal securely.

Cut a small opening in the center of the crust, and insert a "chimney" made of a rolled-up square of parchment or aluminum foil to permit steam to escape. Bake for 30 to 40 minutes, or until crust is rich golden brown. Serve with remaining sauce and more grated Parmesan at table.

Baked Noodles and Cheese

Yield: 4 servings

1 lb medium-wide egg noodles
2 egg yolks
salt
pinch of nutmeg, freshly grated
7 Tb butter
¾ cup grated Swiss cheese
2 Tb bread crumbs

Preheat oven to 375°. Cook noodles in lightly salted boiling water, draining while still slightly underdone. Beat egg yolks together with a pinch of salt and of grated nutmeg. Toss noodles with 4 tablespoons of butter, half the grated cheese, and egg yolks. Mix carefully to blend all ingredients well.

Combine bread crumbs with remaining cheese. Pour noodles into a buttered baking dish, and sprinkle with bread crumb and cheese mixture. Dot with remaining 3 tablespoons of butter, and bake for about 15 minutes, or until hot and bubbly. Serve immediately.

Cheese Ravioli (p. 71)

Cappelletti alla Romagnola (p. 64)

Home-Style Baked Noodles

Yield: 4 servings

Basic Pasta Dough (see Index); or 1 lb long, medium-wide egg noodles (e.g., fettuccine)

8 Tb butter, softened
½ cup grated Parmesan cheese
salt
black pepper, freshly ground
1½ cups bread crumbs
½ lb mozzarella cheese, sliced thin
¼ lb prosciutto (or baked ham), sliced thin

Prepare pasta dough as directed. Next cut dough in long noodles about ¼ inch wide. Cook and drain the pasta, reserving a little of the cooking water. Toss with 4 tablespoons of butter, grated Parmesan, 1 or 2 tablespoons of pasta cooking water, and salt and pepper to taste.

Preheat oven to 400°. Butter an ovenproof dish or a baking pan, and sprinkle with half the bread crumbs. Place half the noodles in the baking dish or pan, and cover with mozzarella and prosciutto. Add the rest of the noodles, dab with remaining 4 tablespoons of butter, and sprinkle with grated Parmesan and rest of the bread crumbs. Bake for 10 minutes, or until lightly browned.

Baked Noodles alla Siciliana

Yield: 4 servings

Basic Pasta Dough (see Index); or 1 lb broad egg noodles

For the sauce and baking:
1 lb lean pork (in 1 piece)
3 slices bacon, chopped (or several slices of fatty ham, chopped)
oil
1 small onion, chopped
1 stalk celery, chopped
1 carrot, chopped
1 garlic clove, chopped
2 lb tomatoes, chopped
salt and pepper
4 hard-cooked eggs, sliced
¾ cup grated Parmesan cheese

Prepare pasta dough as directed, but with 4 cups of flour. Cut dough in strips about 1½ inches wide.

Brown pork and bacon in oil. Add onion, celery, carrot, and garlic, then sauté for 5 minutes. Strain tomatoes through a food mill or sieve, and add to the saucepan. Season to taste with salt and pepper. Add ¼ cup water, and simmer gently for about 2 hours. When the pork is tender, remove from sauce, cool and grind, then return to sauce.

Cook the pasta, and drain while still slightly underdone. Preheat oven to 400°. In a buttered rectangular ovenproof dish, set alternate layers of pasta, meat sauce, slices of egg, and grated Parmesan, finishing with a layer of sauce generously topped with Parmesan. Bake for about 15 minutes, or until lightly browned.

Noodle Casserole with Meat Sauce

Yield: 4 servings

1 lb broad egg noodles

For meat sauce:
1 stalk celery, chopped
1 carrot, chopped
1 small onion, chopped
2 Tb oil
2 Tb butter
¼ lb ground pork
¼ lb sausage meat, crumbled
2 oz mortadella, diced
2 oz cooked ham, diced
salt
¼ cup dry white wine
1½ lb tomatoes, chopped

For Béchamel Sauce and baking:
3 Tb butter
3 Tb all-purpose flour
1 cup milk, heated
½ cup grated Parmesan cheese

Sauté celery, carrot, and onion in oil and 2 tablespoons of butter. Add the ground pork, sausage, mortadella, and ham. Season to taste with salt, stir in wine, and cook over medium heat until wine evaporates. Strain tomatoes through a food mill or sieve, and add to sauce. Bring to a boil, reduce heat, and simmer.

Prepare a Béchamel Sauce: Melt 3 tablespoons of butter, then stir in flour. Add milk gradually and cook, stirring constantly, until sauce thickens. Add salt to taste, and remove from heat.

Preheat oven to 400°. Cook the pasta, and drain while still slightly underdone. Toss with half the meat sauce and half the grated Parmesan. Pour pasta into a buttered ovenproof dish, and cover with rest of the meat sauce and Béchamel. Sprinkle with remaining grated Parmesan, and bake for 15 minutes, or until lightly browned.

Cheese Ravioli

Yield: 4 servings

Dough for Stuffed Pasta (see Index)

For the filling:
1 lb ricotta cheese
1 egg, beaten lightly
3 Tb grated Parmesan cheese
3 Tb minced parsley
salt
black pepper, freshly ground

For the sauce:
Basic Italian Tomato Sauce (see Index)
½ cup grated Parmesan cheese

Prepare stuffed pasta dough as directed.

For the filling: Thoroughly blend ricotta, egg, grated Parmesan, parsley, and salt and pepper to taste.

Prepare ravioli according to instructions given in the Introduction to this section. Cook and drain the ravioli. On a serving platter or in individual plates, alternate layers of ravioli, heated tomato sauce, and grated Parmesan, topping off with a generous sprinkling of cheese.

Ravioli alla Calabrese

Yield: 4 servings

Dough for Stuffed Pasta (see Index)

For the filling:
2 hard-cooked eggs
½ lb mild provolone cheese, minced
½ lb salami, minced
salt and pepper
1 raw egg

For the sauce:
Pork Ragout Sauce (see Index)
¾ cup grated Romano cheese

Prepare stuffed pasta dough as directed.

For the filling: Press hard-cooked eggs through a sieve into a mixing bowl. Add provolone, salami, and salt and pepper to taste. Bind mixture with raw egg.

Prepare ravioli according to instructions given in the Introduction to this section. Cook and drain the ravioli. On a serving platter or in individual plates, alternate layers of ravioli, heated ragout sauce, and grated Romano cheese, topping off with cheese.

Deep-Fried Eggplant Ravioli with Asparagus Tips

Yield: 4 servings

Dough for Stuffed Pasta (see Index)

For the filling:
1 thick slice onion, chopped
6 Tb butter
1 large eggplant, peeled and diced
5 Tb all-purpose flour
1¾ cups milk, heated
2 shelled walnuts, crushed
2 egg yolks, beaten lightly
salt

For deep-frying and serving:
oil
¾ lb asparagus tips
all-purpose flour (for dredging)

Prepare stuffed pasta dough as directed.

For the filling: Sauté onion in butter until it becomes transparent. Add diced eggplant to the skillet. Cook, stirring occasionally, until eggplant is tender. Drain off melted butter into a mixing bowl; add flour and mix thoroughly. Stir in heated milk gradually and blend well. Pour mixture into a saucepan, bring to a boil, reduce heat, then simmer until sauce thickens. Meanwhile, allow eggplant to cool, then mash it well. Remove white sauce from heat, add crushed walnuts and mashed cooked eggplant, and let stand to cool slightly. Stir in egg yolks to bind, and salt to taste.

Prepare ravioli according to instructions given in the Introduction to this section. (Note that for this dish the ravioli should be a bit larger than usual.) In enough hot oil (350°) to cover the ravioli generously, deep-fry them a few at a time. Remove and drain them on paper towels. Then, while keeping the ravioli warm, flour and deep-fry the asparagus tips. Arrange them around ravioli in a serving dish.

Spinach and Ricotta Ravioli with Sage (p. 75)

Sausage Ravioli in Cheese Sauce (p. 75)

Ravioli Gourmet

Yield: 4 servings

Dough for Stuffed Pasta (see Index)

For the filling:
1 thick slice onion, minced
¼ lb fatty prosciutto (or baked ham), minced
2 Tb butter
1 Tb oil
¾ lb ground veal
¼ cup dry white wine
salt and pepper
pinch of nutmeg, freshly ground
beef drippings (optional)
½ cup grated Parmesan cheese
1 egg, beaten lightly

For the sauce:
Bolognese Meat Sauce (see Index)
2 Tb butter, softened
½ cup grated Parmesan cheese

Prepare stuffed pasta dough as directed.

For the filling: Sauté onion and prosciutto in butter and oil until onion becomes transparent. Add ground veal and cook until browned. Stir in wine, bring to a boil, lower heat and simmer until wine evaporates. Season to taste with salt, pepper, and nutmeg. Continue cooking, adding a bit of beef drippings from time to time if necessary. When filling has thickened, remove from heat and add grated Parmesan. Let stand to cool, then blend in egg.

Prepare ravioli according to instructions given in the Introduction to this section. Cook and drain the ravioli. On a serving platter, place alternate layers of ravioli dabbed with soft butter, heated meat sauce, and grated Parmesan, topping off with cheese.

Ravioli alla Napoletana

Yield: 4 servings

Dough for Stuffed Pasta (see Index)

For the filling:
¾ lb ricotta cheese
¼ lb mozzarella cheese, diced
¼ lb prosciutto (or baked ham), diced
¼ cup grated Parmesan cheese
2 Tb chopped parsley
salt and pepper
1 egg, beaten lightly

For the sauce:
Basic Italian Tomato Sauce (see Index)
4 Tb butter, softened
½ cup grated Romano cheese

Prepare stuffed pasta dough as directed.

For the filling: Press ricotta through a sieve into a mixing bowl. Blend in mozzarella, prosciutto, grated Parmesan, and parsley. Season to taste with salt and pepper, then bind with the egg.

Prepare ravioli according to instructions given in the Introduction to this section. Cook and drain the ravioli. On a serving platter, place alternate layers of ravioli dabbed with softened butter, warmed tomato sauce, and grated Romano, topping off with cheese.

Sausage Ravioli in Cheese Sauce

Yield: 4 servings

Dough for Stuffed Pasta (see Index)

For the filling:
1 thick slice onion, minced
2 Tb butter
¾ lb sausage meat (or patties)
¾ cup bread crumbs
salt and pepper
2 egg yolks
3 Tb grated Parmesan cheese

For the sauce:
6 Tb butter, softened
¾ cup grated Parmesan cheese
⅔ cup heavy cream, heated

Prepare stuffed pasta dough as directed.

For the filling: Sauté onion in butter until it becomes transparent. Crumble sausage meat over onion, stir, and continue to sauté until the sausage is well done. Add bread crumbs, season to taste with salt and pepper, and cook for another 10 minutes. Remove from heat, and let stand to cool. Add egg yolks and grated Parmesan, blending well.

Prepare ravioli according to instructions given in the Introduction to this section. Cook and drain the ravioli when still slightly underdone. Preheat oven to 400°. In a buttered ovenproof serving dish, arrange alternate layers of ravioli, dabbed with soft butter, and grated Parmesan, reserving a few tablespoons of cheese. Pour hot (but not boiling) heavy cream over the top, then sprinkle with remaining Parmesan. Bake for 10 to 15 minutes, or until nicely browned.

Spinach and Ricotta Ravioli with Sage

Yield: 4 servings

Dough for Stuffed Pasta (see Index)

For the filling:
1 lb fresh spinach (or 10-oz pkg chopped frozen)
¾ lb ricotta cheese
½ cup grated Parmesan cheese
salt and pepper
pinch of nutmeg, freshly grated
1 egg, beaten lightly

For the sauce:
¼ lb butter
3 or 4 fresh sage leaves (or pinch of dried sage)
1 cup grated Parmesan cheese

Prepare stuffed pasta dough as directed.

For the filling: Boil spinach in a little lightly salted water. Drain and squeeze out all the water, then chop spinach and let stand to cool. Press ricotta through a sieve, and mix with spinach and grated Parmesan. Season to taste with salt, pepper, and nutmeg. Stir in beaten egg to bind.

Prepare ravioli according to instructions given in the Introduction to this section. Cook the ravioli; then, a few minutes before they are done, melt butter in a small skillet or saucepan together with sage leaves. Drain the ravioli, and remove the sage leaves from melted butter. In a deep serving dish, place alternate layers of ravioli, sage butter, and grated Parmesan, topping off with cheese.

Vegetarian Ravioli

Dough for Stuffed Pasta (see Index)

For the filling:
2 large eggplants
oil
½ cup shelled walnuts
3 Tb butter .
2 Tb all-purpose flour
1 cup milk
2 Tb chopped parsley
¾ cup grated Parmesan cheese
salt
pinch of nutmeg, freshly grated
2 egg yolks, beaten lightly

For the sauce:
Basic Italian Tomato Sauce (see Index)
½ cup grated Parmesan cheese

Prepare stuffed pasta dough as directed.

For the filling: Peel and dice eggplant, and sauté in enough oil to come about ⅛ inch up the sides of the skillet. Drain the cooked eggplant in a sieve, and let stand to cool. Then mince eggplant and walnuts together. Next, in a small saucepan, melt butter over medium heat. Add flour and cook, stirring until well blended. Meanwhile, bring milk almost to a boil; pour it into flour mixture, stirring constantly, and continue cooking until thick and smooth. Set aside to cool slightly, then combine with parsley, grated Parmesan, and a pinch of salt and nutmeg. Stir in the eggplant-walnut mix, and add egg yolks to bind.

Prepare ravioli according to instructions given in the Introduction to this section. Cook and drain the ravioli. In a deep serving dish, set alternate layers of ravioli, warmed tomato sauce, and grated Parmesan, topping off with cheese.

Timbale Cups alla Napoletana

Basic Pasta Dough (see Index)

For the sauce and baking:
6 Tb butter
6 Tb all-purpose flour
2 cups milk, heated
salt and pepper
½ lb mozzarella, diced
½ lb prosciutto (or baked ham), diced
¼ lb salami, diced
½ cup bread crumbs

Prepare pasta dough as directed, but with only 2 cups of flour; then cut in thin strips. Let dry on a flat surface.

Prepare a Béchamel Sauce: Melt 4 tablespoons of butter, and stir in flour. Gradually add milk, stirring constantly. Season to taste with salt and pepper, then cook, stirring, until sauce thickens. Remove from heat.

Preheat oven to 400°. Cook the pasta and drain while still slightly underdone. Toss with Béchamel Sauce and diced mozzarella, prosciutto, and salami. Butter muffin cups with 2 tablespoons of melted butter, coat with bread crumbs, and fill with pasta mixture, pressing firmly into the cups. Bake for about 15 minutes, or until light golden crusts form. Let cool slightly, then unmold on a serving platter.

Macaroni Meat Pie with Mushrooms (p. 68)

Timbale with Eggplant

Yield: 6 servings

For the pie crust:
3 cups all-purpose flour
1 tsp salt
10 Tb shortening
1 egg

For the filling:
2 large eggplants
4 Tb oil
salt
1 garlic clove, minced
1 lb tomatoes, chopped
pinch of basil
¾ lb large elbow macaroni
3 Tb butter
⅓ cup grated Parmesan cheese

For the pie crust: Sift flour and salt into a mixing bowl, and cut in shortening with a pastry blender. Add egg and mix with the hands, handling dough as little as possible. Sprinkle with a little cold water if necessary to make a smooth, elastic ball. Refrigerate dough for 30 minutes.

Preheat oven to 425°. Roll the dough out about ¼ inch thick. Butter a deep round cake pan or baking dish, and line it with the dough. Pierce bottom in several places with a fork. Roll out the dough trimmings, and cut out a circle the diameter of the pan; pierce with a fork, and place on a buttered cookie sheet. Bake bottom crust and top circle for 12 to 15 minutes, or until pale gold in color. (Do not allow pastry to brown.)

For the filling: Cut eggplant in strips, and sauté in 3 tablespoons of oil. Sprinkle with salt to taste. In another pan, sauté minced garlic in 1 tablespoon of oil, then add tomatoes, basil, and salt to taste, and simmer until sauce thickens.

Cook the pasta, and drain while still slightly underdone. Toss with tomato sauce, butter, and grated Parmesan. Spoon a third of sauced pasta into pie shell, cover with half the sautéed eggplant, continue with another third of pasta, remaining eggplant, and final portion of pasta. Level the mixture in the pie shell, cover with the pie-crust circle, and bake for about 15 minutes at 375°, or until pastry is a rich golden brown.

Index of Recipes by Category